THE
IROQUOIS

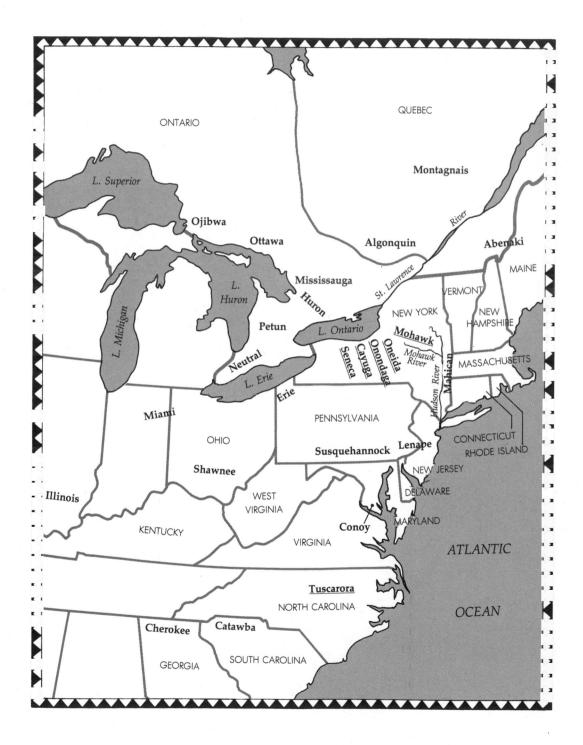

QUEBEC

ONTARIO

Montagnais

L. Superior

Ojibwa

Ottawa   Algonquin   Abenaki

River

Mississauga   MAINE

L.   Huron   *St. Lawrence*   VERMONT
Huron   NEW
                                      NEW YORK   HAMPSHIRE
L. Michigan

Petun   *L. Ontario*   **Mohawk**

Neutral   **Seneca** **Mohawk**   MASSACHUSETTS
                               Cayuga *River*
                        L. Erie **Onondaga** **Mahican**
                               Oneida

                        Erie

Miami   PENNSYLVANIA   CONNECTICUT
                                                           RHODE ISLAND
        OHIO   **Lenape**
                               Susquehannock
Shawnee   NEW JERSEY

Illinois   DELAWARE

        WEST   *Hudson River*
        VIRGINIA

        KENTUCKY   **Conoy**   MARYLAND

                        VIRGINIA   **ATLANTIC**

                Tuscarora

                NORTH CAROLINA   **OCEAN**

        Cherokee   **Catawba**

        GEORGIA   SOUTH CAROLINA

INDIANS OF NORTH AMERICA

THE IROQUOIS

Barbara Graymont
Nyack College, New York

Frank W. Porter III
General Editor

CHELSEA HOUSE PUBLISHERS
New York   Philadelphia

On the cover Washington Covenant wampum belt, made when George Washington was president and believed to commemorate a peace agreement between the Six Nations of the Iroquois and the 13 original American colonies. More than 6 feet long, this is the longest wampum belt known to exist today.

Chelsea House Publishers
Editor-in-Chief Nancy Toff
Executive Editor Remmel T. Nunn
Managing Editor Karyn Gullen Browne
Copy Chief Juliann Barbato
Picture Editor Adrian G. Allen
Art Director Giannella Garrett
Manufacturing Manager Gerald Levine

Indians of North America
Senior Editor Marjorie P. K. Weiser

Staff for **THE IROQUOIS**
Copy Editors Terrance Dolan, Karen Hammonds
Deputy Copy Chief Ellen Scordato
Editorial Assistant Tara P. Deal
Senior Designer Laurie Jewell
Picture Researcher Susan Quist
Production Coordinator Joseph Romano

Copyright © 1988 by Chelsea House Publishers, a division of Main Line Book Co. All rights reserved.
Printed and bound in the United States of America.

5 7 9 8 6 4

Library of Congress Cataloging in Publication Data

Graymont, Barbara.
The Iroquois / Barbara Graymont.
   p. cm.—(Indians of North America)
Bibliography: p.
Includes index.
ISBN 1-55546-709-1
      0-7910-0361-2 (pbk.)
1. Iroquois Indians. I. Title. II. Series: Indians of North
America (Chelsea House Publishers)   88-3038
E99.I7G66   1988   CIP
970.004'97—dc 19   AC

CONTENTS

INDIANS OF NORTH AMERICA

CHELSEA HOUSE PUBLISHERS

INDIANS OF NORTH AMERICA: CONFLICT AND SURVIVAL

Frank W. Porter III

The Indians survived our open intention of wiping them out, and since the tide turned they have even weathered our good intentions toward them, which can be much more deadly.

John Steinbeck
America and Americans

When Europeans first reached the North American continent, they found hundreds of tribes occupying a vast and rich country. The newcomers quickly recognized the wealth of natural resources. They were not, however, so quick or willing to recognize the spiritual, cultural, and intellectual riches of the people they called Indians.

The Indians of North America examines the problems that develop when people with different cultures come together. For American Indians, the consequences of their interaction with non-Indian people have been both productive and tragic. The Europeans believed they had "discovered" a "New World," but their religious bigotry, cultural bias, and materialistic world view kept them from appreciating and understanding the people who lived in it. All too often they attempted to change the way of life of the indigenous people. The Spanish conquistadores wanted the Indians as a source of labor. The Christian missionaries, many of whom were English, viewed them as potential converts. French traders and trappers used the Indians as a means to obtain pelts. As Francis Parkman, the 19th-century historian, stated, "Spanish civilization crushed the Indian; English civilization scorned and neglected him; French civilization embraced and cherished him."

Nearly 500 years later, many people think of American Indians as curious vestiges of a distant past, waging a futile war to survive in a Space Age society. Even today, our understanding of the history and culture of American Indians is too often derived from unsympathetic, culturally biased, and inaccurate reports. The American Indian, described and portrayed in thousands of movies, television programs, books, articles, and government studies, has either been raised to the status of the "noble savage" or disparaged as the "wild Indian" who resisted the westward expansion of the American frontier.

Where in this popular view are the real Indians, the human beings and communities whose ancestors can be traced back to ice-age hunters? Where are the creative and indomitable people whose sophisticated technologies used the natural resources to ensure their survival, whose military skill might even have prevented European settlement of North America if not for devastating epidemics and the disruption of the ecology? Where are the men and women who are today diligently struggling to assert their legal rights and express once again the value of their heritage?

The various Indian tribes of North America, like people everywhere, have a history that includes population expansion, adaptation to a range of regional environments, trade across wide networks, internal strife, and warfare. This was the reality. Europeans justified their conquests, however, by creating a mythical image of the New World and its native people. In this myth, the New World was a virgin land, waiting for the Europeans. The arrival of Christopher Columbus ended a timeless primitiveness for the original inhabitants.

Also part of this myth was the debate over the origins of the American Indians. Fantastic and diverse answers were proposed by the early explorers, missionaries, and settlers. Some thought that the Indians were descended from the Ten Lost Tribes of Israel, others that they were descended from inhabitants of the lost continent of Atlantis. One writer suggested that the Indians had reached North America in another Noah's ark.

A later myth, perpetrated by many historians, focused on the relentless persecution during the past five centuries until only a scattering of these "primitive" people remained to be herded onto reservations. This view fails to chronicle the overt and covert ways in which the Indians successfully coped with the intruders.

All of these myths presented one-sided interpretations that ignored the complexity of European and American events and policies. All left serious questions unanswered. What were the origins of the American Indians? Where did they come from? How and when did they get to the New World? What was their life—their culture—really like?

In the late 1800s, anthropologists and archaeologists in the Smithsonian Institution's newly created Bureau of American Ethnology in Washington, D. C., began to study scientifically the history and culture of the Indians of North America. They were motivated by an honest belief that the Indians were on the verge of extinction and that along with them would vanish their languages, religious beliefs, technology, myths, and legends. These men and women went out to visit, study, and record data from as many Indian communities as possible before this information was forever lost.

8

By this time there was a new myth in the national consciousness. American Indians existed as figures in the American past. They had performed a historical mission. They had challenged white settlers who trekked across the continent. Once conquered, however, they were supposed to accept graciously the way of life of their conquerors.

The reality again was different. American Indians resisted both actively and passively. They refused to lose their unique identity, to be assimilated into white society. Many whites viewed the Indians not only as members of a conquered nation but also as "inferior" and "unequal." The rights of the Indians could be expanded, contracted, or modified as the conquerors saw fit. In every generation, white society asked itself what to do with the American Indians. Their answers have resulted in the twists and turns of federal Indian policy.

There were two general approaches. One way was to raise the Indians to a "higher level" by "civilizing" them. Zealous missionaries considered it their Christian duty to elevate the Indian through conversion and scanty education. The other approach was to ignore the Indians until they disappeared under pressure from the ever-expanding white society. The myth of the "vanishing Indian" gave stronger support to the latter option, helping to justify the taking of the Indians' land.

Prior to the end of the 18th century, there was no national policy on Indians simply because the American nation had not yet come into existence. American Indians similarly did not possess a political or social unity with which to confront the various Europeans. They were not homogeneous. Rather, they were loosely formed bands and tribes, speaking nearly 300 languages and thousands of dialects. The collective identity felt by Indians today is a result of their common experiences of defeat and/or mistreatment at the hands of whites.

During the colonial period, the British crown did not have a coordinated policy toward the Indians of North America. Specific tribes (most notably the Iroquois and the Cherokee) became military and political pawns used by both the crown and the individual colonies. The success of the American Revolution brought no immediate change. When the United States acquired new territory from France and Mexico in the early 19th century, the federal government wanted to open this land to settlement by homesteaders. But the Indian tribes that lived on this land had signed treaties with European governments assuring their title to the land. Now the United States assumed legal responsibility for honoring these treaties.

At first, President Thomas Jefferson believed that the Louisiana Purchase contained sufficient land for both the Indians and the white population.

Within a generation, though, it became clear that the Indians would not be allowed to remain. In the 1830s the federal government began to coerce the eastern tribes to sign treaties agreeing to relinquish their ancestral land and move west of the Mississippi River. Whenever these negotiations failed, President Andrew Jackson used the military to remove the Indians. The southeastern tribes, promised food and transportation during their removal to the West, were instead forced to walk the "Trail of Tears." More than 4,000 men, women, and children died during this forced march. The "removal policy" was successful in opening the land to homesteaders, but it created enormous hardships for the Indians.

By 1871 most of the tribes in the United States had signed treaties ceding most or all of their ancestral land in exchange for reservations and welfare. The treaty terms were intended to bind both parties for all time. But in the General Allotment Act of 1887, the federal government changed its policy again. Now the goal was to make tribal members into individual landowners and farmers, encouraging their absorption into white society. This policy was advantageous to whites who were eager to acquire Indian land, but it proved disastrous for the Indians. One hundred thirty-eight million acres of reservation land were subdivided into tracts of 160, 80, or as little as 40 acres, and allotted to tribe members on an individual basis. Land owned in this way was said to have "trust status" and could not be sold. But the surplus land—all Indian land not allotted to individuals— was opened (for sale) to white settlers. Ultimately, more than 90 million acres of land were taken from the Indians by legal and illegal means.

The resulting loss of land was a catastrophe for the Indians. It was necessary to make it illegal for Indians to sell their land to non-Indians. The Indian Reorganization Act of 1934 officially ended the allotment period. Tribes that voted to accept the provisions of this act were reorganized, and an effort was made to purchase land within preexisting reservations to restore an adequate land base.

Ten years later, in 1944, federal Indian policy again shifted. Now the federal government wanted to get out of the "Indian business." In 1953 an act of Congress named specific tribes whose trust status was to be ended "at the earliest possible time." This new law enabled the United States to end unilaterally, whether the Indians wished it or not, the special status that protected the land in Indian tribal reservations. In the 1950s federal Indian policy was to transfer federal responsibility and jurisdiction to state governments, encourage the physical relocation of Indian peoples from reservations to urban areas, and hasten the termination, or extinction, of tribes.

Between 1954 and 1962 Congress passed specific laws authorizing the termination of more than 100 tribal groups. The stated purpose of the termination policy was to ensure the full and complete integration of Indians into American society. However, there is a less benign way to interpret this legislation. Even as termination was being discussed in Congress, 133 separate bills were introduced to permit the transfer of trust land ownership from Indians to non-Indians.

With the Johnson administration in the 1960s the federal government began to reject termination. In the 1970s yet another Indian policy emerged. Known as "self-determination," it favored keeping the protective role of the federal government while increasing tribal participation in, and control of, important areas of local government. In 1983 President Reagan, in a policy statement on Indian affairs, restated the unique "government to government" relationship of the United States with the Indians. However, federal programs since then have moved toward transferring Indian affairs to individual states, which have long desired to gain control of Indian land and resources.

As long as American Indians retain power, land, and resources that are coveted by the states and the federal government, there will continue to be a "clash of cultures," and the issues will be contested in the courts, Congress, the White House, and even in the international human rights community. To give all Americans a greater comprehension of the issues and conflicts involving American Indians today is a major goal of this series. These issues are not easily understood, nor can these conflicts be readily resolved. The study of North American Indian history and culture is a necessary and important step toward that comprehension. All Americans must learn the history of the relations between the Indians and the federal government, recognize the unique legal status of the Indians, and understand the heritage and cultures of the Indians of North America.

Tadodaho, the most powerful and feared Iroquois chief of legendary time, an Onondaga, sculpted of soapstone in 1980 by Cleveland Sandy, a Cayuga of Six Nations Reserve.

1

THE
TIME
OF
TROUBLES

In the land south of Lake Ontario, along the Mohawk River and westward to the Finger Lakes and Genesee River, in what is now New York State, there lived five related but separate Indian nations. To the Europeans who would later come into their territory, they would be known as the Mohawks, Oneidas, Onondagas, Cayugas, and Senecas. Collectively, the newcomers would refer to these Indians as the Iroquois. Each nation lived in its own separate territory, in several villages built in forest clearings and tightly stockaded for protection against attacks from enemies.

To the east, along the Hudson River, were the Mahicans, longtime enemies of all the Iroquois people. The Mohawks, the Iroquois whose territory was nearest, bore the major burden of this ongoing warfare. Fierce on the warpath, the Mohawks attacked not only the Mahicans but also the Abenakis and other New England Indians in the east and the Algonquian-speaking tribes in

the north. The Mohawks were always feared. They called themselves Ganiengehaka, "People of the Place of the Flint," or, as they are generally called, "People of the Flint Country." But so devastating were they on the warpath that their enemies gave them the name by which they have since become known—Mowak (Mohawk)—"Man Eaters."

Warfare was a way of life for all of the Iroquois nations. So often did the sun shine down upon men fighting that it was said in those days that the sun loved war. The power and the prestige of the warriors increased with each battle. They had become so attached to war and the glory it brought them that they could not give it up.

The Iroquois tribes not only made war upon their enemies but, most unfortunately, even upon one another. Attacks by a war party of one Iroquois nation upon the village of another would lead to reprisals, revenge, and long years of blood feud. Fear and

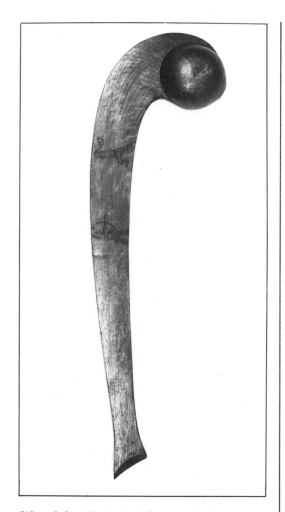

War club with incised figures of two fighting Indians. War clubs were carved from ironwood and were about 2 feet long; the ball head is about 6 inches in diameter.

hatred were the normal feelings of each Iroquois nation for the others. Even in his own village, a warrior could not always trust his neighbor. People used to say that when the clouds were hiding our Grandmother the Moon, it was not safe to wander about by night.

The most famous and most feared of these warriors was Tadodaho, a chieftain of the Onondaga nation. He was intelligent, crafty, and evil. He had the appearance of a cruel and ugly monster, with hair matted and twisted, like snakes encircling his head. Tadodaho's reputation as a mighty warrior and a powerful wizard attracted a group of young men who followed him, eager to do his bidding. When those who had opposed him died mysteriously or were driven away from the village, the Onondaga people became terrified. They whispered among themselves that Tadodaho could destroy people even when he was not present. His strength and cunning, his abilities as a sorcerer, and his reputation for cannibalism effectively silenced those who wished to see peace among all peoples.

Tadodaho and his warriors intimidated their own Onondaga people and terrorized the nearby Cayuga settlements and the Seneca villages farther west. At night people had frightful dreams of being tortured and murdered. The whole Iroquois country was fast becoming a wasteland.

Among the Onondagas, there was a courageous leader who had no fear of Tadodaho. The good chief Hayenwatha had frequently tried to reform the evil war leader and straighten his crooked mind. Tadodaho refused to accept the advice or leadership of any man. He regarded Hayenwatha's peacemaking efforts with contempt.

Hayenwatha loved his people more than his own safety. Determined to continue his campaign for peace, he sent messages to all the Onondaga villages inviting the people to attend a grand council. There he would present his proposals for peace, friendship, and cooperation. When the day arrived, a large crowd assembled around the council fire. The people waited expectantly. They hoped the great orator Hayenwatha would give them good news, that the time of troubles would end so they could henceforth live without fear.

As the meeting was about to begin, Tadodaho appeared, angry and ferocious. He said not a word, but his presence shadowed the gathering. The people saw his ruthless warriors scattered throughout the crowd. So great was the fear that those who opposed Tadodaho would be murdered by him or his followers that no one dared debate. The council was a failure.

Not long afterward, Hayenwatha's eldest daughter became sick and died. Her illness did not respond to the skill of any healer. People were convinced that her death was due to Tadodaho's witchcraft.

If Hayenwatha had been more cautious or more cowardly, he might have retired to his own home, attended solely to family affairs, and given up his great plan for peace. But this good man knew that a chief must be ready to make great sacrifices for the welfare of his nation. Accordingly, he did not hesitate to send runners out again to call the villagers to a second council.

This meeting was no more successful than the first. Fewer people at-

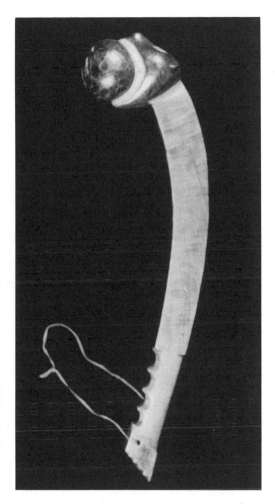

A war club with a panther head and turtle on the handle. Used to give a hammer blow or thrown with stunning accuracy, the war club was a formidable weapon.

tended and most again shuddered with fear at the presence of Tadodaho and his warrior band. Once more the people departed with nothing accomplished.

After the second council, the second of Hayenwatha's daughters died in the same manner as her elder sister. Was it

Creations Battle, *painted in acrylics in 1980 by John Fadden, Mohawk, Onchiota, New York, shows the struggle between the Good Twin and the Evil Twin at the time of Creation.*

THE IROQUOIS STORY
OF CREATION

Long before there were human beings, there were Sky People. They dwelled in the celestial world. In those days there was no sun. All light came from the large white blossoms on the celestial tree that stood in front of the Lodge of the Sky Chief. This Sky Chief had married a young wife. In time this wife, Sky Woman, began to show signs that she would soon bear a child.

There was a troublesome being, called Firedragon, in the Sky World. Firedragon was always spreading rumors. Now he whispered to Sky Chief that the child who was about to be born would not be his. In a fit of anger and jealousy, Sky Chief uprooted the great celestial tree in front of his lodge. He pushed his wife through the hole where the tree had once stood.

Sky Woman fell rapidly down toward the vast dark waters below. The birds, feeling sorry for her, flew underneath and gently supported her, breaking her fall and carrying her slowly downward. At the same time, the water animals hurried to make a place for her. Turtle said that he would support a world on his back. The sea animals plunged down into the water looking for some earth. Muskrat succeeded and came up with a large mouthful of earth, which he placed on Turtle's back. The light from the blossoms of the fallen celestial tree shone through the hole where it had stood and became the sun. When Sky Woman landed, everything was in readiness for her, with grass and trees beginning to grow.

Sky Woman gave birth to a daughter. When this daughter grew to womanhood, she began to be with child. No one knows whether her husband was Turtle or West Wind, but she gave birth to two remarkable twin boys—one good and one evil. The Good Twin was born in the usual way. But the Evil Twin was in a hurry and pushed through his mother's side to be born. In doing so, he killed his mother.

Sky Woman buried her daughter, and plants miraculously began to grow from various parts of the daughter's body—a tobacco plant, a cornstalk, a bean bush, and a squash vine. This was the origin of all the plants that would be most important to the human beings who would come later.

The Good Twin and the Evil Twin quickly grew to manhood. As soon as they were grown, they proved true to their names. The Good Twin began creating all sorts of good things: plants, animals, medicinal herbs, rivers, and streams. The Evil Twin began to spoil his brother's work, putting rapids and boulders in the rivers, creating poisonous plants, thorns and briars, diseases, and monsters. The Good and Evil Twins fought against each other to see who would predominate in creation, but the Evil could never overcome the Good. Finally the Good Twin created human beings to enjoy all the good things he had made for them. And that is how it all began.

a coincidence? Now people were certain that it was Tadodaho's doing, that it was a contest of will and power between two great men—one evil and one good. How long could evil continue to overcome good?

For Hayenwatha, the work of reform was becoming not only difficult but highly dangerous. Only sorrow and more tragedy lay ahead as he tried to carry out his responsibility as a faithful chief. He refused to abandon his struggle, however. After the burial of his second daughter and the end of the period of mourning, he called a third council.

The youngest daughter of Hayenwatha accompanied her father to this council. She was his beloved and his greatest delight—not only was she the only surviving member of his family, but she was soon to make him a grandfather. As the council delegates began to gather, she went to the edge of the clearing with the other women to help collect firewood for cooking. Busy with her task, she paid little attention to the assembly.

Suddenly a great eagle appeared, gracefully gliding over the treetops and circling the clearing where the delegates were coming together. Tadodaho was the first to see him. Pointing upward, he cried out to his most skilled warrior to shoot. The man immediately sent an arrow flying from his bowstring and killed the eagle as it flew.

The great bird fell to earth next to Hayenwatha's daughter. With a shout of delight, the warriors rushed forward to pluck the valuable feathers from the

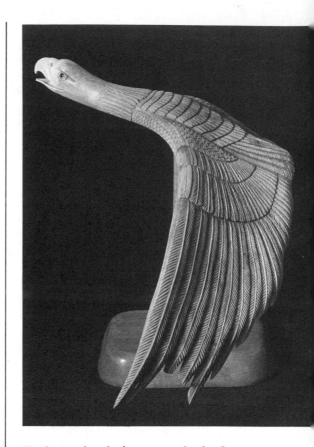

Eagle, *sculpted of moose antler by Stan Hill, a Mohawk from the Six Nations Reserve, in 1980. The eagle, one of the national symbols of the Iroquois, is often shown atop a pine tree calling out a warning that enemies are approaching.*

fallen eagle. In their haste to claim their prize, they unthinkingly knocked down the helpless young woman and trampled her to death.

The grief-stricken Hayenwatha had now lost the remaining member of his family and was left alone in the world. His most beloved daughter lay dead upon the field, still carrying within her the child who would never be born. As the people gathered around in horror and remorse, Hayenwatha mournfully cried out, "I have now lost all my daughters and in the death of this, my last daughter, you have accidentally and unwittingly killed two beings."

Having met only frustration and despair in trying to bring peace to his people, Hayenwatha left his Onondaga village. Overcome with grief and rage, he plunged into the forest and became a lonely wanderer. On his long and sorrowful journey, his grief began more and more to distort his mind.

Completely alone and constantly grieving, he felt that goodness had left him and that he had taken on the characteristics of Tadodaho, his adversary. His face, once kindly, now grew dismal and frightening. In the depths of his depression he became convinced that he was a cannibal. His mind was no longer straight. In his enormous grief, it had become crooked.

On the pathway of sorrow he had only nature for a companion. No fellow human ever came to lift his burden from him. It was to nature that he began to look for relief.

One morning as he wandered on his way, he saw a stand of rushes growing before him. He cut a quantity of the jointed rushes and strung them together into three strings of beads. Then he cut two forked sticks and thrust their long ends into the ground. He placed a pole across the forked angle of the sticks and sat down before them. Then he placed his three strings over the pole and said to himself: "This would I do if I found anyone burdened with grief even as I am. I would console them for they would be covered with night and wrapped in darkness. This would I lift with words of condolence and these strings of beads would become words with which I would address them."

This, the later Iroquois would say, was the origin of the condolence ritual, by which mourners even today are comforted and relieved of their sorrow.

As Hayenwatha turned eastward in his journey, he came to an area of small lakes. On the shores he saw numerous small white shells. He picked them up and strung them together. Then he put the several strings of white shells around his neck as a sign of peace, for he was entering the land of the Mohawks, the People of the Flint Country.

When he reached the edge of the forest on the outskirts of one of the Mohawk villages, he sat down upon the stump of a fallen tree. Soon a young woman came out of the village carrying an elm-bark bucket to get water from a nearby spring. When she saw Hayenwatha sitting there quietly, she returned to her village and related the news. "A man, or a figure like a man, is seated by the spring, having his breast covered with strings of white shells."

At this time a man from the north, Deganawidah, was living in the village. He had come to the Mohawks with a message of peace. He knew that the stranger came as a friend, for the white shells were emblems of peace. He

The Grief of Ainwatha (*Hayenwatha*), *painted in acrylics by John Fadden, Mohawk, Onchiota, New York, in 1983. Mourning his daughters, Hayenwatha holds condolence strings.*

therefore sent a messenger to welcome Hayenwatha and escort him into the village.

As Hayenwatha accompanied his escort into the village of long bark-covered lodges, he felt friendship all about him. These Mohawks, so feared by their enemies, lived among themselves in a kindly manner. The escort took the

visitor to the lodge of Deganawidah, who rose to greet Hayenwatha. Even before they spoke, the two men understood each other.

"My younger brother," said Deganawidah, "I perceive you have suffered from some deep grief. You are a chief among your people and yet you are wandering about."

Hayenwatha told his host of his great sorrow in the loss of his entire family and related to him the bitter experience of his wandering and his loneliness.

"Dwell here with me. I will represent your sorrow to the people who live here," Deganawidah assured him.

As he promised, Deganawidah laid all the sad troubles he had heard before the chiefs in council. Their hearts were touched, and they sent Deganawidah to lift their guest's burden.

When Deganawidah returned to his lodge, he heard Hayenwatha mourning before the three strings of beads on the pole before him. He thereupon approached his new friend and took up the strings to condole with him.

Presenting the first string, Deganawidah said: "When a person has suffered a great loss caused by death and is grieving, the tears blind his eyes so that he cannot see. With these words, I wipe away the tears from your eyes so that now you may see clearly."

Presenting the second string, he said: "When a person has suffered a great loss caused by death and is grieving, there is an obstruction in his ears and he cannot hear. With these words

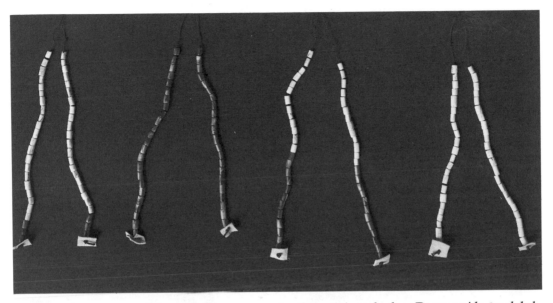

Strings of wampum used in condolence ceremonies that originated when Deganawida condoled Hayenwatha after the deaths of his daughters.

I remove the obstruction from your ears so that you may once again have perfect hearing."

Presenting the third string, he said: "When a person has suffered a great loss caused by death, his throat is stopped and he cannot speak. With these words, I remove the obstruction from your throat so that you may speak and breathe freely."

These are the basic "three words" of the condolence ceremony, observed by the Iroquois even to this day.

With this ceremony, Hayenwatha's mind became straight once again.

He looked upon Deganawidah and thought he had never seen such goodness and kindness before. Surely, he felt, the Master of Life must have led him to this place and to this man.

In turn, Deganawidah saw in Hayenwatha a strong and righteous man, with many talents and abundant courage. He had been searching for such a companion to help him in his mission of peace. Together they could spread the Good News to all the nations.

Here among the People of the Flint Country, Hayenwatha found a new home, a new life, and a great work. ▲

The Council with Tadodaho When the League was Started, *a 1936 tempera painting by Seneca artist Ernest Smith. The Iroquois history and cultural traditions have provided rich subject matter for tribal artists in the 20th century.*

THE GREAT PEACE

Deganawidah had also been a lonely wanderer before coming to the Mohawk village. He had been born in the land of the Wendot people, a tribe north of Lake Ontario. These people, whom the French would later call Hurons, were distantly related to the Iroquois tribes south of the lake. Their way of life was similar, even though they spoke a slightly different language. Like the Iroquois, the Wendots honored their women, especially women who had borne children. Among both peoples it was the mothers who chose the chiefs and the mothers who could remove the chiefs from office if they failed in their duties. Every child belonged to the family line of his or her mother.

The women tended to the household duties and did the farming. They raised huge quantities of corn, beans, and squash, which composed the main food supply of the Iroquoian people. Together this triad of vegetables was known as "Our Supporters" or "The Three Sisters."

All Iroquois men were hunters and warriors, supplementing the food supply and protecting the villages from attack. Since ancient times, the Wendots had made war against neighboring tribes and especially against their distant kin, the Iroquois south of Lake Ontario. Every young man was expected to do his duty as a warrior and protector of his people.

Young Wendot boys played at war to sharpen the skills they would need later in life, but as he was growing to manhood, Deganawidah talked only of peace, friendship, and unity. This handsome young man was always strictly honest and always spoke with a straight tongue. To the Wendots, however, he was strange. He had departed from the way the Wendots considered that a young man should go, and his talk was foolishness. Most people believed that the only way to have peace was to smash all enemies, to attack and destroy them before they destroyed you. The grown men regularly went off on war expeditions. The

Wendots were of one mind that Deganawidah was not accepting his proper role as a man among them. Furthermore, although he held no office in his nation, he gave people advice on how to live and how to govern, causing resentment and jealousy. Moreover, he claimed that his message of peace had come to him directly from the Master of Life.

Deganawidah's ideas and actions were noticeably separating him from his people. The Wendots could not understand a man who loved peace more than war. They could not tolerate one whom they had known since childhood presenting himself to them as a prophet. So great was their animosity toward him that Deganawidah at last came to feel that his message would be better received by other people, far from his home.

After he came to this decision, Deganawidah built a canoe and fondly took leave of his mother and grandmother. He told them that it was time for him to depart and search out the council smoke of far-flung nations in order to preach his message of peace. "It is my business," he told them, "to stop the shedding of blood among human beings."

He then set out on Lake Ontario, paddling south toward the far shore to the land of the five Iroquois nations. When he reached his destination, he saw some men along the shore running to him. When they came close, he asked what they were doing in that lonely place. They replied that they were hunters far from their own village because of troubles at home.

Deganawidah directed them to go back to their village and announce to their chief that the Great Peace had come and that their village would now be free of troubles. "And if he asks you from whence came the Good Tidings of Peace and Power," Deganawidah continued, "you will say that the Messenger of the Good Tidings of Peace and Power will come in a few days."

When they asked him his name, Deganawidah responded, "It is I who came from the west and am going eastward and am called Deganawidah in the world."

As he had instructed them, the hunters returned to their village to announce to their chief that the Good News of Peace and Power had come. They related their meeting with Deganawidah and said that he would soon arrive at their settlement. The chief expressed great pleasure and satisfaction at the news, for his village had long been troubled.

On his way toward the hunters' settlement, Deganawidah stopped at the small bark lodge of a woman who lived alongside the warriors' path that ran from east to west. It was her custom to greet and feed the warriors whenever they passed by her house on their errands of destruction. She also greeted and fed Deganawidah.

After eating, Deganawidah explained to her the Good News of Peace and Power. "I carry the Mind of the Master of Life and my message will bring an end to the wars between east and west." He instructed her that henceforth she must cease feeding the warriors. "The Word that I bring is that all peoples shall love one another and live together in peace."

"That is indeed a good message," the woman responded. "I take hold of it. I embrace it."

This woman became the first person to accept the Great Peace. Deganawidah therefore named her Jigonsasee, or New Face, because she reflected the New Mind. He appointed her to be the Mother of Nations, the Great Peace Woman, and told her, "I now charge you that you shall be the custodian of the Good Tidings of Peace and Power, so that the human race may live in peace in the future."

Deganawidah then continued on his journey eastward toward the Flint Country, and made his way to one of the Mohawk villages. There he sat down at the edge of the forest and began to smoke his pipe. This was the custom for a visitor approaching a strange village, so he would not startle the people, who might otherwise mistake him for an enemy.

When men from the village came to question him, he explained that he was on a mission of peace and so they took him to their chiefs. After presenting his peace message to the chiefs, he offered it to all the people of the village. The Mohawks had suffered greatly from war and welcomed this proposal for friendship, which would mean unity and justice among all peoples.

A wooden pipe with bowl cover, carved with masks and an animal figure. Pipe bowls were usually carved of soapstone (steatite); one made of wood is unusual.

Among the Iroquois tribes, the code of honor required revenge for a life taken. Killing always led to more killing, and the cycle of revenge thus meant perpetual war. If one tribe had proposed peace to another, it would have been considered cowardice and weakness. There seemed to be no way out of this bloody dilemma.

Now this tribeless man, Deganawidah, came to the Mohawks with a plan to end their troubles. Without a tribe of his own, he was neutral. He had never been involved in any of the killing. Because no man's hand was against him, he could become a peace messenger among the tribes without disgrace or accusation of cowardice. The Mohawks therefore gladly took hold of his message and became the first nation to accept the Great Peace.

It was after Deganawidah had prepared the minds of the People of the Flint Country for the Good News that Hayenwatha arrived and was condoled by Deganawidah. After his mind had become straight, Hayenwatha was accepted into the Mohawk nation and became one of its chiefs. In their different ways, each of these two men had tried to promote peace. Now they joined together to strengthen their work and spread the message of peace far beyond their village.

What they proposed was the formation of a confederation, or family, of nations. Each tribe that accepted the Good News of Peace and Power would become a nation within the confederation. Together they would be known as the League of the Iroquois. To design the government for the confederation, they drew on a structure that was already familiar to them. The league would become an extended family, based on the local kinship groups known as clans.

The most basic unit of Iroquois society was a group of relatives that traced its descent from a single woman. In the Mohawk language, this group was called the *ohwachira*. The eldest woman of each ohwachira was generally its head. Two or more ohwachiras made up a clan, and everyone in a clan considered every other clan member to be a relative. Because of this relationship, marriage within a clan was forbidden. Occasionally a clan had only one ohwachira, usually because the other ohwachiras in that clan had died out.

A person was born into his or her clan, inheriting the family and clan affiliation of his or her mother. A stranger like Deganawidah or Hayenwatha, or a war captive, could be incorporated into the tribe by adoption. Adoptees would take on the identity of the family and clan that adopted them and thereby become full-fledged members of the tribe. Adoption was the Iroquois method of conferring citizenship.

Each clan had as its name and symbol a certain bird or animal. The Mohawks and the Oneidas had only three clans: Turtle, Wolf, and Bear. These three clans were also present among the Onondagas, Cayugas, and Senecas; but these three tribes had other clans as well, such as Snipe, Heron, Beaver, Deer, Eel, and Hawk. Each clan was entitled to a certain number of chiefs, and the head mothers of the ohwachiras chose the chiefs for their own particular clan. Each clan governed itself and also joined with the other clans in governing the village and the tribe.

HOW A LEGEND
WAS MADE

In the mid-19th century, Henry Rowe Schoolcraft, a government agent among the Indians of the upper Great Lakes, began writing down the folklore and legends of the Ojibwa Indians, including the tale of the demigod Nanabozho. He also began collecting material for his 1846 book, *Notes on the Iroquois*, and acquired from the New York author J. V. H. Clark stories · relating to Chief Hayenwatha, or Hiawatha, as the name was sometimes written. In ignorance, Schoolcraft applied the name of the Iroquois chief to Nanabozho and published the result in *The Hiawatha Legends*. The poet Henry Wadsworth Longfellow became acquainted with Schoolcraft's writings and was inspired to compose a long poem about the exploits of Nanabozho and his companions under the mistaken impression that he was writing about a hero named Hiawatha. Longfellow's fanciful poem, "The Song of Hiawatha," though a moving and beautiful literary creation, had nothing whatsoever to do with the noted Iroquois chieftain and only served to obscure and confuse this leader's very great achievements.

An illustration for "The Song of Hiawatha," 19th century.

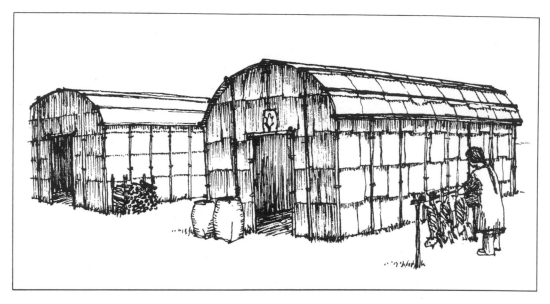

An elm bark longhouse, the traditional dwelling of the Iroquois. The turtle over the doorway indicates the clan of the residents.

It was this clan government that Deganawidah and Hayenwatha planned to apply to the whole confederacy they hoped to establish. The clan chiefs would become the confederacy chiefs, but the government of the confederation would not interfere with the independence of the clan or tribal governments.

The Great Peace, or *Kayanernh-kowa*, that Deganawidah and Hayenwatha established would have three parts, each with a double meaning:

The Good Word, which is righteousness in action, bringing justice for all.
Health, which is a sound mind in a sound body, bringing peace on earth.
Power, which is the establishment of civil authority, bringing with it the increase in spiritual power in keeping with the will of the Master of Life.

After the Mohawks accepted the plan of the confederacy, they directed Deganawidah and Hayenwatha to send messengers to their neighbors to the immediate west, the Oneidas, the People of the Standing Stone. There the messengers were to lay the proposal before the leading chief, Odatshedeh.

After he listened to the messengers' explanation of the Great Peace, Odatshedeh replied, "I will consider this plan and answer you tomorrow."

The messengers clearly understood that "tomorrow" meant "next year," for the Iroquois always gave long and serious consideration to every important proposal.

After a year had passed, the Oneida council sent word that they would take hold of the Great Peace. A treaty was therefore concluded between the Oneidas and the Mohawks, which laid the foundation of the League of Peace.

The next people to the west were the Onondagas. They were willing to accept the offer of Deganawidah and Hayenwatha, but their powerful chief Tadodaho refused. Despite this setback, the delegation journeyed on to the next nation, the Cayugas.

When the Cayugas heard of the proposal for peace, unity, and power, they accepted the offer with great relief. For many years they had suffered from the attacks of the powerful Onondagas. Now they felt the strength and security the League of Peace would give them.

The ambassadors then proceeded farther west to the Genesee River and the land of the Senecas, the People of the Great Hill. Here, too, they would have a problem. Various factions among the Senecas prevented the nation from reaching a unanimous decision.

The Seneca chiefs replied to Deganawidah: "We lords on either side of the river have decided to accept your message which you left. The only difficulty which we have now to contend with is that our chief warrior and his deputy have failed to agree with us to accept the message, and they have the power to control the people, and we lords on either side of the river are totally be-

The Hiawatha Belt, probably the most important Iroquois wampum, symbolizes the formation of the League. The pine tree in the center represents the League; the joined rectangles symbolize the several nations. The belt was damaged and is now incomplete.

wildered and fail to see a way out of the difficulty."

Deganawidah encouraged the Senecas to settle their problems, and he accepted those chiefs who had grasped the Good News. With the confederacy growing stronger with every passing year, he was confident that a way would soon be found to persuade the unwilling portion of the Senecas to join the movement for unity.

Then Deganawidah and Hayenwatha turned their attentions back to the Onondagas, where Tadodaho remained coldly opposed to the confederation. They determined to win the reluctant chief over with a combination of spiritual power, a curing ceremony, and political persuasion.

A delegation from the newly formed League went to the Onondagas, with a singer in front singing a peace hymn and other sacred songs that Deganawidah had taught. The Onondaga chiefs welcomed them and took them to the lodge of Tadodaho. There Deganawidah sang the peace hymn before the evil-minded chieftain and, after he had finished, rubbed down Tadodaho's body in a sacred medicine ceremony. All Iroquois, even those who were antisocial or malicious, believed in the reality of the supernatural and in the power of the medicine ceremonies to cure the mind and the body. The people watched closely to see if the sacred herbs and the ritual would produce the desired effect on their chief.

Deganawidah then explained to Tadodaho that the assembled people rep-resented all the nations united in a strong league, but that they wished to lay their heads before him. It was a metaphor for submission, meaning that they would all recognize him as their leading chief. Tadodaho was silent.

Another chief then spoke, indicating the chiefs, warriors, and the Peace Woman, Jigonsasee, who were present: "The lords and all the chief warriors and this great woman, our mother, have all agreed to submit the Good Tidings of Peace and Power to you, and thus if you approve and confirm the message, you will have the power and be the Fire-Keeper of our Confederate Council, and the smoke from it will rise and pierce the sky, and all the nations will be subject to you."

Then Tadodaho broke his silence and said, "It is well. I will now answer the mission which brought you here. I now truly confirm and accept your message, the object of which brought you here."

Tadodaho's mind had now been made straight.

It still remained to convince that portion of the Senecas who followed war chiefs to come into the League. This was accomplished when the confederate chiefs and warriors unanimously decided to make the two Seneca war chiefs the war captains of the confederacy, to lead the Five Nations in case of attack and to command the defense of the confederacy. The Seneca war chiefs accepted this offer and Deganawidah pronounced the power of the League to be "full and complete."

An old Indian trail in Seneca territory, near Conesus Lake, New York. The Iroquois lived in an environment of fertile forest land, punctuated with numerous lakes and rivers.

 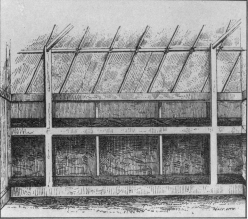

Views of the outside and inside of an elm bark longhouse were drawn for Lewis Henry Morgan's 1851 book about the Iroquois. The steeply sloping roof was unusual at that time and may have been inspired by the homes of non-Indians who settled in Iroquois country.

Deganawidah chose as a symbol of the League of the Five Nations the pine tree, the Tree of the Great Long Leaves. The tree had four symbolic roots, the Great White Roots of Peace, spreading north, east, south, and west. If any other nation ever wished to join the League, it would have to follow the White Roots of Peace to the source and take shelter beneath the tree. Atop the tree, he placed an eagle to scream out a warning at the approach of danger. He symbolically planted the tree in the land of the Onondagas, the place of the Great Council Fire. There the confederate lords, or peace chiefs, would sit beneath it and be caretakers of the Great Peace. And these lords, the chiefs, would figuratively never die, because their chiefly titles would be passed down to their successors forever. In this way, the League of the Five Nations would always be kept alive.

The Iroquois also referred to the Great Peace, or the confederacy, as the Extended Lodge, or *Kanonghsionni* in the Mohawk language. The name was a reference to the long, bark-covered lodges in which multiple related families lived in their villages. This family lodge now figuratively became even longer, or extended, so that it covered the entire country of the Five Nations, binding all its inhabitants together as one family.

After completing his work, Deganawidah instructed the people never to pass his name down to another and never to speak it again except in ritual use or when the Great Peace was being discussed. Accordingly, out of respect, Deganawidah in later years was generally referred to by Iroquois speakers as "The Man from the North" or "The Peacemaker." The names of all the other founding chiefs, including that of

Hayenwatha, would be inherited by their successors in their respective clans.

No one today knows exactly when the Confederacy of the Five Nations was founded. We know only that when the Europeans first met the Iroquois, their confederacy was already very old. The 17th-century Jesuit missionaries referred to the League of the Five Nations as "ancient." Horatio Hale, a 19th-century scholar who gave the subject much study, put the date of the founding at approximately A.D. 1459.

The history of the League's founding had been handed down orally among the Iroquois for hundreds of years. After several 19th-century non-Indian scholars such as Horatio Hale and Lewis Henry Morgan began to publish articles and books about Iroquois history, ritual, and culture, a number of knowledgeable Iroquois themselves undertook to write down the story of the origin of the League. Each person who told the story, however, told it in a different way. There were many versions and no two accounts agreed about every detail or even about the order of events. As the tale was recounted in every village year after year, over a period of perhaps 500 years, fact had become much mixed with legend. This transformation of the historical account shows the extent to which these events had taken on a sacred character for the Iroquois. The exact details were not nearly as important to them as testifying to the authenticity of their confederacy and the significance of what their ancestors had done for them. In establishing unity and preserving their nationhood, the ancestors had provided for all time a purpose in life and a way of life for the people of the Extended Lodge. ▲

Stone Giant Emerging, *soapstone sculpture by Joseph Jacobs,*
Cayuga, Tuscarora Reservation, 1978. The stone giants of Iroquois
tales were the most feared of the evil monsters of ancient times.
Neither arrows nor spears could pierce their stone coats.

THE
EXTENDED LODGE
FLOURISHES

The establishment of the League of the Five Nations strengthened and protected them from enemies on the outside and ensured their ongoing peaceful coexistence within. They shared their hunting grounds with one another and the men hunted in peace. The women tilled the fields around their villages and planted crops, confident that any enemies were too far away to disturb their homeland.

The Creator had given them the Three Sisters, Our Supporters—corn, beans, and squash. First they planted the corn in the fields in small hills about three feet apart, row upon row. When the young corn plants came up, the women planted bean or squash seeds in the same hills. These crops, which came up later, would twine around the cornstalks. This method of planting, which kept the bean and squash vines off the ground, made it easy to hoe the weeds and harvest the crops. When the soil around a village became exhausted, usually in 10 or 15 years, the people moved to a more promising site. After the initial effort of rebuilding their homes and clearing and tilling the fields, they adjusted easily to the new locale.

For the Iroquois, as for tribal people generally, religion was an inseparable part of daily life. Spiritual powers were everywhere in the natural world, and people always sought to keep in the right relationship to them. The Iroquois were grateful to the Creator and the benevolent supernaturals for their help. Knowledge of how to perform the proper rituals and ward off evil forces was essential. In every season of the year, great ceremonies were held to give thanks for the bounties of nature. These occasions unified the community in a common purpose and way of life.

One of the oldest of the agricultural observances was the Green Corn Festival, held at the time the corn, beans, and squashes became ripe, when the people rejoiced and gave thanks for their good fortune. In later years, when agriculture became even more prominent in their lives, the Iroquois

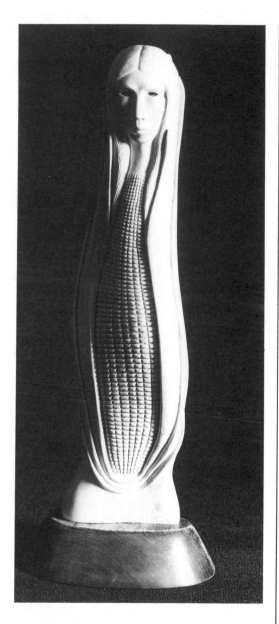

Corn Spirit, *sculpted of moose antler by Stan Hill, Mohawk of the Turtle Clan, Six Nations Reserve, Ontario, Canada, 1984. Corn, beans, and squash, the most important crops of the Iroquois, were referred to as the Three Sisters or Our Supporters.*

developed a cycle of agricultural thanksgiving ceremonials. At planting time and as the various berries and crop plants ripened, from the time the maple sap flowed in early spring to the final gathering of the crops in late fall, there was a joyous round of thanksgiving services. A ritual leader recited thanksgiving chants, the people performed religious dances to the accompaniment of rattle or drum, and the entire community feasted to mark all these observances.

In winter, after the men returned from the fall hunt, the Iroquois held their great New Year's or Mid-Winter Festival, called "The Most Excellent Faith" in their language. This was a time of renewal and cleansing—a cleansing of people's spirits and a ritual cleansing of their homes. On the opening day, the elders who were the keepers of the faith went to every home in the village to announce the beginning of the festival. They instructed all residents to clean their homes, visit their neighbors, and stir the ashes on their hearths. Then the people went around the village with small paddles, visiting their neighbors and stirring the ashes in each home. The faith keepers also visited homes to stir the ashes and give thanks to the Creator for preserving the people through the year. There is evidence that at one time the people extinguished the old fires in their homes and kindled new ones as a symbol of renewal. In more recent times, the new-fire rite has fallen into disuse and only the ash-stirring rite continues.

An essential part of the Mid-Winter Festival was the practice of dream guessing. The Iroquois regarded dreams as important communications from supernatural beings. For this reason it was necessary that any instructions given in a dream be followed. People who had a dream to be guessed would describe it in a disguised fashion, requiring their neighbors to guess the actual content and then to satisfy the dreamer's desires. With satisfaction received, the troubled minds of the dreamers were restored to wholeness.

Two Jesuit missionaries who witnessed the Mid-Winter Festival at Onondaga in 1656 described the ceremony. Some of the dreamers who came into their cabins behaved in a most extreme manner, singing, shouting, dancing, and threatening, demanding that their dreams be guessed and satisfied. Others were more subdued in their requests. One of these was a woman who came in and quietly laid down a mattock, or digging hoe. The people guessed that she was asking for a plot of land. "That was just what she had in mind," reported the Jesuits, "and she was satisfied with five furrows for planting Indian corn."

In assessing the importance of this dream-guessing ceremony for the community, the Jesuits explained: "It would be cruelty and a sort of murder not to give a man what his dream called for, for the refusal might cause his death. Therefore they may see themselves stripped of their all without any hope of recompense. For whatever they give

A Cayuga water drum, used at dance rituals. In the 19th century drums were made from such containers as butter tubs and commercial leather. The drum's pitch depends on the level of water in the container and the tightness of the skin.

is never returned to them, unless they dream it themselves, or pretend to dream it. In general, they are too scrupulous to make such a pretense, which would, as they suppose, cause all sorts of misfortunes."

To the Jesuits, the entire ceremony was offensive and foolish; but they apparently understood its deep significance to the Iroquois. This dream guessing served a major purpose of releasing tension in the community. Long before the development of the modern science of psychology, the Iroquois recognized that illness could be caused by the mind as well as by natural forces (such as injuries) or by witchcraft. Disorders of the mind were, they believed, often caused by unconscious desires, which might be revealed to a person in a dream. To make the ill person well again, it was essential for a dream wish to be fulfilled, either actually or symbolically. A dream of hostility against a member of the community was always fulfilled symbolically rather than in actuality. In this way, the peace and unity of the village were preserved and the dreamer was satisfied.

Modern psychotherapy, drawing on methods developed just a century ago, makes use of dreams as an aid in revealing unconscious desires and emotional problems. According to anthropologist Anthony F. C. Wallace, who studied the Iroquois wish-dreams in the 1950s, the Iroquois achieved "a great deal of psychological sophistication" in making this discovery independently and several centuries earlier.

In the wintertime also, after the earth had died and when the spirits that guarded the growing things were asleep, the people liked to sit around their fires and tell ghost stories and tales of the supernaturals. One favorite story was of the carnivorous (meat-eating) skeleton who chased lonely travelers at night in order to eat them. You could sometimes hear this fiend's hollow moan in the stillness of the night. There were also stories of flying heads, bodiless creatures, big and frightful, darting rapidly through the air with their long hair streaming around them. Other tales told of the exploits of a race of stone giants, the most feared of all monsters, that used to wander about the countryside in olden days doing evil and even eating people.

The storytellers also fascinated their listeners with accounts of the Naked Bear and the warrior who overcame him, of the Great Horned Serpent, the Monster Mosquito, witches, and talking animals. There was no end to these marvelous tales of terror, wonder, and courage. The folklore of the Iroquois people was part of their children's traditional education. They learned all the stories at an early age and in later years would pass them down to their own children and grandchildren.

The supernatural world was also very near when healing arts were practiced. Physical illness, the Iroquois believed, could be caused not only by natural means but also by witchcraft and evil spirits. Different types of healers were necessary to treat these various diseases, although a particular medicine man or woman might use several methods of treatment. Herbalists and surgeons used natural remedies to treat the natural causes of their patients' disorders. They treated familiar maladies such as coughs, fevers, agues (severe fever or chill), rattlesnake bites, wounds, and broken bones by probing and cleaning the wounds, setting the bones, using salves, emetics, or other medicines that they had made themselves, as the situation demanded. They had considerable skill and remarkable knowledge of the healing properties of a vast number of plants.

The False Faces arrive to purify a longhouse to prevent illness. This ceremony, known as the Traveling Rite, was traditionally held in the spring and fall. A person wearing a pig mask and costume walks on all fours alongside the procession of medicine society members. This is one of a series of drawings illustrating Iroquois customs by Jesse Cornplanter, Seneca, 1903.

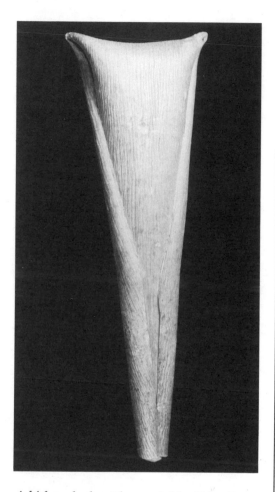

A hickory bark rattle, carried by False Faces in certain ceremonies. These rattles were made from pliable bark folded on itself like an envelope. When dry the bark was tightly sealed. Wild cherry pits were placed inside.

The conjurers, as the Europeans later called them, attempted to cure through the use of magic arts, by singing ritual medicine songs or incantations to counteract witchcraft and by blowing and sucking over the affected part of a patient's body. Healers who used this latter technique would withdraw from their mouths a hair, splinter, stone, or some other object that they claimed to have sucked out of the sick person's body and announce that this was the cause of the illness. Everyone assumed that the patient had been under the spell of some witch and was now relieved by the healer's counter-magic, as evidenced by removal from the patient's body of a foreign object placed there by the witch. This type of exorcism usually had a beneficial psychological effect upon the patient, as well as on members of his or her family.

Other healers had special power to counteract the work of those evil supernaturals who sought to harm humans and spread discord and chaos in the world. For lack of a more precise term in our own language, we refer to them as shamans, or priests.

Some healers combined all these skills. Even herbalists believed in the power of magic and would often use it in combination with natural remedies when treating patients. Those who were skilled in the mysteries of medicine were believed to possess sacred knowledge.

From ancient times the Iroquois had had medicine societies, composed of healers and those who had been cured by the ceremonies of the members. There might be several such societies, each having its own rituals and cures, in any village. When members of some of these medicine societies performed their curing ceremonies, they might wear masks portraying various supernaturals. The masks represented sacred power and were held in high esteem by the Iroquois.

The most important Iroquois ritual commemorates the formation of the confederation, the Good News of Peace and Power. The memory of this great episode, the central event of their history, is preserved in the Condolence Council. This ritual takes place after a chief dies, when his successor, chosen by the head women of the clan, is raised to chiefly office as a lord of the confederacy. The condolence for a chief, which is still carried on by the Iroquois today, is far more elaborate than the family condolence for a person of lesser rank. This great ceremony is a confederacy-wide event and includes a recitation of the chiefly names of all the earliest lords of the confederacy. The titles exist and are in use to this day. Their recitation means that the confederacy and its leadership will always remain intact. The Condolence Council is a eulogy to those whose wisdom and energy established the League, a ceremony of comfort for mourners from the family and clan of the deceased, a ritual to replace the one who has died, and a means of ensuring for all time the continuance of the work of the Founding Fathers.

In this ceremony, the antlers of a buck deer are placed upon the head of the new chief as the symbol of his office and power. According to tradition, Deganawidah had explained the practice in the following words: "The reason why we do this is because all people

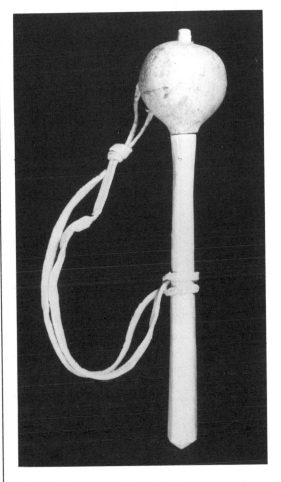

A gourd rattle used in planting ceremonies and at the medicine society meetings known as "pumpkin shakes." A gourd is a pumpkin-like plant that dries to form a firm container.

live upon the flesh of the deer, and the reason that we take the emblem of the deer horns is that this institution, the Great Peace, shall be the means of protecting our children hereafter."

As with all peoples who had no writing system, the Iroquois depended upon memory to preserve and the spoken word to pass down their history, traditions, and rituals. This required prodigious feats of memory, for many of the major legends were extremely lengthy, running to 75,000 words or more. The ritualists and archivists of the Five Nations who possessed this large store of essential knowledge were the intellectuals of their communities, equivalent in status to any learned European priests and professors.

As an aid to memory, the Iroquois in later years used shells and shell beads. The Europeans called the beads wampum, from *wampumpeag*, a word used by Indians in the area who spoke Algonquian languages. According to the Iroquois tradition, Hayenwatha was the originator of wampum, but archaeological evidence shows that shell beads were in widespread use by the Iroquois and other Indians long before the formation of the Five Nations Confederacy. However, the more elaborate wampum "belts," with figures or designs on them, made for use in treaty negotiations and as historical records, seem to have been a later development among the Iroquois.

The type of wampum most commonly used in historic times was bead wampum. It was laboriously cut from various seashells, ground and polished, and then bored through the center with a small hand drill. Most wampum was made from the quahog, or large hardshell clam. The Indians of Long Island, in southern New York, were the chief producers of wampum and paid huge quantities of it in tribute, showing that they accepted the superior power of the Iroquois.

The Iroquois strung the beads and wove them into broad multirowed straps or belts for use in various ceremonies and in diplomacy. Strings of mourning wampum were used in condolence ceremonies to remove the grief from those who had lost a family member. Chiefs possessed wampum as a sign of their office. Strings and belts of wampum were used to convey messages in diplomatic relations and to represent the articles of treaties. A messenger who did not present wampum as a pledge of the truth of his words would not be taken seriously. Belts were also used to record great events in Iroquois history. The beads, purple and white, were arranged in designs to represent the event the belt was commemorating.

Certain elders were designated to memorize the various events and treaty articles that the belts represented. Those men could "read" the belts and reproduce their contents with great accuracy. These important belts were stored at Onondaga, the capital of the confederacy, in the care of a designated wampum keeper.

Life was good to the people of the Five Nations for generations after the confederation. They continued to prosper and generally to enjoy the blessings of nature. Nature was generous and the people were industrious. Iroquois culture was vigorous and dynamic.

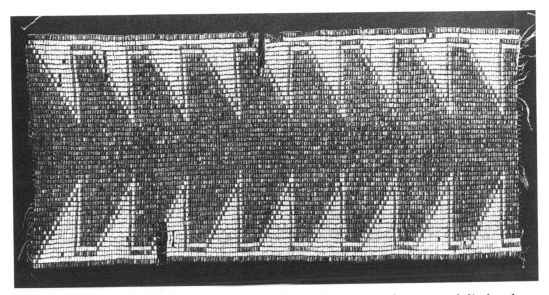

The Wing or Dust Fan wampum belt, held by the council of the confederacy and displayed whenever the League's constitution was recited. Purple beads form the ever-growing pine tree, symbolic of the life of the League. This is the widest wampum belt known.

The confederacy was a remarkable creation, formed by an early people, showing their great political and social sophistication. They were kindly and reverent, affectionate and loyal toward their families, considerate and tender toward their friends. They had provided within their League a means for extending the house and admitting other peoples into their peaceful way of life. In later years, other Indian tribes would accept this offer and take shelter beneath the Tree of the Great Long Leaves. The Five Nations prospered as a result of their unity. Unfortunately, the surrounding nations did not also benefit from the Great Peace. The Iroquois felt no security on their borders when neighboring nations rejected the confederacy or thwarted their interests. Even after the formation of the League, intermittent raids on the fringes of its borders continued. In later years, these conflicts often became furious beyond belief as the League sought to extend its peace by means of warfare. ▲

Tree of Peace Pot, *a clay vase by Sara Smith, Mohawk, Six Nations Reserve, 1979. Above the tree the eagle screams out a warning. The roots stretch in all directions, and a club is buried under the tree, where the groundwater can carry away weapons.*

IROQUOIS
AND
EUROPEANS

People everywhere aspire to an ideal but must daily deal with realities. So it was with the Iroquois. The ideal was that the Great Peace should extend to all humanity. The reality was that it had to be a peace on Iroquois terms, within the confines of their political and social structure. Because the surrounding peoples did not all agree to this, warfare would continue, killing of enemies would continue, grief would continue, and retaliation would continue in order to dry the tears of the mourners.

The formation of the League had settled the problem of blood feuds among the five tribes and had brought a general peace to their territory. The issue of how to handle murders or accidental killings of Iroquois by other confederacy members was now to be resolved by the murderer or his family giving gifts, particularly wampum, to the victim's relatives. As a result of this solution, the incessant retaliatory feuds would cease and the people of the confederacy would live together in a spirit of friendship and cooperation.

There were some problems, however, that the establishment of the Great Peace did not solve. Hostilities within the group were now unacceptable and so aggressions had to be directed outward. Warfare was one of the major means by which the men, and particularly the young men, achieved fame, prestige, and power. Hunting and fishing, also male occupations, likewise brought prestige but could take place only at certain seasons of the year. Moreover, the women, who were the farmers and gatherers of nuts and wild berries, supplied a large amount of the food. Thus they shared in the prestige of being nurturers of the village. At certain periods during the year, there was little for the men to do in times of peace. A man's advancement within his community depended upon his skills and achievements, and the successes of the warrior upon the field of battle assured for him the admiration and gratitude of his village. Warriors also served an important social function in bringing back captives to be adopted to replace dead relatives or sacrificed to please certain supernatural beings. One of these supernaturals, Agreskwe, required a gift of the first fruits of the hunting and fishing seasons and the first enemy warriors captured in a year.

Continued warfare thus met an important social and religious need among the Iroquois, even after the founding of the League of Peace. The League, in fact, now made it possible for the Five Nations to direct their energies outward against their neighbors not only in defensive wars but, after the coming of the Europeans, in a long series of conquests of neighboring peoples that led to almost perpetual war in the 17th and 18th centuries.

The object of traditional Indian warfare had been largely to achieve prestige, seek revenge, plunder, or take captives, and with the least loss of life to the attacking party as possible. Originally, Indian warfare was not conducted with the severe intensity of European wars. Objectives were often limited ones. Indians, the Iroquois included, considered it foolish to fight gloriously to the last man when their war parties could successfully withdraw from a raid or battle and live to fight another day. Early European observers of Indian campaigns, misunderstanding their nature, described them as more sport than serious conflict.

The coming of the Europeans profoundly changed the nature of Iroquois warfare. An economic motive now became predominant as tribes competed

Jacques Cartier, the 16th-century French explorer, is shown looking at a map of the St. Lawrence River.

for hunting territories and supplies of beaver skins to trade for the European goods that were rapidly becoming important in their lives.

In 1534, Jacques Cartier and his band of French explorers came to Canada and journeyed along the St. Lawrence River on the first of three voyages to that region. First the French encountered some Algonquian-speaking Indians, then farther upriver some villages of presently unidentifiable Iroquoian speakers. By the early 17th century, these St. Lawrence Iroquois had totally disappeared. Cartier and his men established trade relations with the Indians who lived along the river and entered into friendly alliances with the Algonquian-speaking Indians of that area, particularly the Algonquins and Montagnais who lived north and west of the St. Lawrence River. Some French trade goods began to reach other tribes through regular Indian trade networks and through enemy raids on the Algonquins and Montagnais.

Long before they met the French, the Iroquois had begun to acquire French trade goods through warfare with the Indians of the St. Lawrence River. Metal goods, such as axes, were particularly desirable to the Iroquois. Like their neighbors, they had only tools they made themselves from stone, bone, and shells. It was largely the Mo-

hawks, the easternmost of the Iroquois nations, who participated in these raiding expeditions along the St. Lawrence.

By 1609, these raids were disrupting the French and Indian fur trade in the St. Lawrence area. Samuel de Champlain, the governor of New France and founder of the settlement of Quebec, decided to help his Indian trading partners in a campaign against the Mohawks. With a few Frenchmen and 60 warriors from the Algonquin, Montagnais, and Huron nations, Champlain headed south down the Richelieu River and over the lake that now bears his name. At the southern end of Lake Champlain, on the evening of July 29, they encountered a party of 200 Iro-

Lake Champlain, the scene of the first battle in which the Iroquois faced French firearms.

The French, with muskets, and their Indian allies, with bows and arrows, attack the stockade surrounding an Iroquois village from both a siege tower and the ground.

quois warriors in canoes. The Iroquois landed and immediately began to fortify their position, while their French and Indian opponents remained close together on the lake in their canoes.

It was Indian custom not to fight at night. The Iroquois said that the sun liked to see their courage. Both sides therefore spent the night preparing for the next day's battle, shouting insults at each other and boasting of their own bravery. Champlain and his two French companions kept hidden in the Montagnais canoes during the night.

At daybreak, the Montagnais, Algonquins, and Hurons landed and rushed at the Iroquois, who were gathered by their fort. Suddenly the attackers' formation divided and Champlain moved to the front. He wore a suit of half armor and an open-faced metal helmet and carried a matchlock-style musket. The Iroquois, who wore slatted wooden body armor for protection in

FALSE AND HUSK FACES

Sacred tobacco was burned as an offering to a living basswood tree before the first carving for a False Face was done into it. Only sincere and pure men could "ask the life" and carve masks that would contain the life spirit of a tree.

Wood masks, or False Faces, and cornhusk masks, or Husk Faces, are an important part of Iroquois religious practice. The Faces represent spirit beings that have the power to heal.

The Iroquois view illness as a disorder of the natural world caused by evil supernatural beings. The Faces symbolize spirits that bring order and restore health. They share their healing power with humans in exchange for gifts of Indian tobacco and cornmeal, human possessions that these spirits value.

In the spring and fall of every year, the False Faces perform the Traveling Rite to cleanse their village. They publicly visit the homes of all religious traditionalists on the reservation and ceremonially sweep diseases out of their houses. People give the maskers gifts of Indian tobacco. Then the Faces and members of the community go to the longhouse, the traditionalists' place of worship, for additional rituals and a feast in honor of the Faces. At such ceremonial feasts, foods that the supernaturals are believed to like are served: Hominy (cornmeal mush) and corn soup are preferred by False Faces; popcorn and cornmeal cakes baked with huckleberries, by Husk Faces.

When medicine society members wear False Faces or Husk Faces in curing rituals and religious ceremonies, they portray supernaturals and thus become endowed with their power. Both men and women who have been cured become members of the Society of Faces, but only the men wear masks and cure.

Many modern Iroquois oppose public display of the sacred False Faces and believe that they should be used only in religious ceremonies.

49

Above: *Old Broken-Nose, carved in 1937 by Elon Webster, Onondaga. Different mask types symbolize various supernaturals. Old Broken-Nose represents a powerful being whose face was injured by a moving mountain.*
Left: *Old Broken-Nose, an older Onondaga Face. It is said that this supernatural taught an exhausted hunter to carve masks from a living tree and perform the rituals.*

Above: *The Hunch-back, carved in 1943 by Robert T. Hatt, Cayuga, Six Nations Reserve, Canada. Bags of sacred tobacco attached to a mask indicate successful curing rituals.*

Right: *Seneca buffalo or devil mask, with pointed, hornlike leather ears. Iroquois masks usually have large, prominent lips, a possible reference to the practice of blowing hot ashes on an ill person during a curing ritual.*

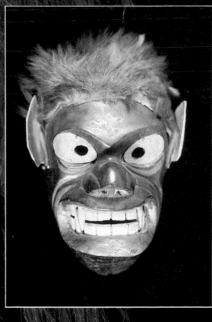

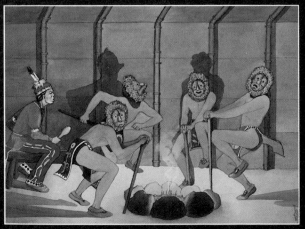

Husk Faces, also called "bushy head" or "fuzzy hair" masks, represent the supernaturals who taught humans how to hunt and farm. They are made by women from braided dried cornhusks. Above: Seneca miniature Husk Face, 4 1/4 x 4 3/4 inches, made in the 1970s. Left: Fuzzy Hair Society, watercolor by Ernest P. Smith. The artist wrote: "They are cousins of the False Face and have the same curing powers. They talk only in whispers and carry a staff to fend off all evil."

At the Six Nations Reserve,
Husk Faces are always men.
On Seneca reservations in
New York, women may wear
masks in certain Husk Face
dances, but only the men of
the society perform the cures.
Above: *Seneca Husk Face
made by Mattie Young, 1970s.*
Right: *Cayuga Husk Face
made by Sayehwas, about
1932.* **Far right:** *Husk Face,
Grand River Reservation.*

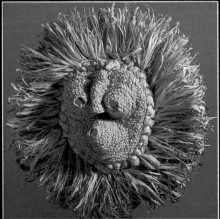

Left: *Harvest mask with cornhusks and horsehair, Onondaga, New York, probably made about 1870.*

Above: *Scalp mask, Oklahoma Seneca.*

Left: *Wolf clan mask, about 1775. Said to have belonged to Joseph Brant, this is one of the earliest Faces known.*

Above: *Whirlwind mask, Cayuga, Grand River Reservation. The extended tongue is believed to show pain. Some say that the divided face, represents a half-human, half-supernatural creature.*

Members of the False Face Society visit traditionalists'
homes during the Mid-Winter Festival. They stir ashes on
the hearths and, if the residents wish, perform curing
rituals. The Faces also conduct special ceremonies and
dances at the longhouse for the benefit of all present.
Above: Laughing Beggar Face, Seneca, worn by boys who
visit homes and beg for tobacco at the Mid-Winter
Festival. **Left:** Messengers known as "Our Uncles the Big
Heads" arrive at a house. Watercolor by Jesse
Cornplanter, Seneca, about 1901.

battle, hesitated and stared in astonishment at this bearded creature in shiny clothing coming toward them. Before the Iroquois could recover from their surprise and let loose a hail of arrows, Champlain fired his musket at the three war chiefs whom his allies had pointed out to him. Two Mohawk chiefs were killed instantly and a third lay mortally wounded. Another Frenchman, concealed behind a tree, also fired into the group of Mohawks.

This first encounter with European firearms caused havoc among the Iroquois, and the Montagnais and their allies soon had them on the run. The attackers killed about 50 of the fleeing Iroquois and took 12 prisoners. It was a victory that firmly sealed the friendship of the French and the Indian tribes of Canada and began decades of alternating deadly conflict and diplomatic peace between the Iroquois and the French.

Another encounter between the two sides, the Battle of the Richelieu, on June 19, 1610, was even more significant than the previous year's Battle of Lake Champlain. Huron and Algonquin hunters, coming to trade their beaver pelts with the French, detected 100 Mohawk warriors building a wooden fort along the Richelieu River. Montagnais traders, who had set up a temporary camp at the mouth of the river where it enters the St. Lawrence River, heard of this discovery. They sent to the French for military assistance to help punish the Mohawks. Champlain complied and departed with the Montagnais and a small party of Frenchmen.

At first the battle went badly for the attackers. The Mohawks repulsed a charge on their fort, killing a number of war chiefs in the process. They had devised a strategy of avoiding the French musket fire by dropping to the ground while the bullets sailed harmlessly overhead. Champlain, accustomed to the siege warfare tactics practiced in Europe, now instructed his Indian comrades to use their shields for protection and move forward to attach ropes to the supporting logs of the fort while the French covered them with musket fire. When they pulled on the ropes, the logs toppled and the walls of the fort collapsed. When the breach in the walls was successfully made, the attackers rushed forward, killing more than 80 Mohawks and taking the remainder prisoner.

The Indian and French victory would mean an end to Iroquois raids in the St. Lawrence valley for many years. Events to the south and east would occupy the Iroquois in the very near future.

At about the same time, the Dutch began exploring and settling along the Hudson River, and a new avenue of trade opened to the Indians of that region. Fort Orange and the upper Hudson River, site of present-day Albany, was the center of the Dutch-Indian fur trade. Unfortunately for the Mohawks, the Mahicans lived between them and the Hudson River and so were the first to benefit from the Dutch presence. Both Mahicans and Mohawks were determined to monopolize trade with the Dutch, which led to the reopening of the old Mohawk-Mahican War.

The Mohawk also attacked the Abenaki in Maine and the Algonquian-speaking tribes of southern New England. The Mohawks thus opened up a new line of trade for themselves with the English settlers in this region.

In 1626, in the early phases of the Mohawk-Mahican War, the Mohawks defeated a Dutch-Mahican war party that had invaded their territory. When a Dutch trader from Fort Orange went to the Mohawks to renew friendship with them, they scolded him and the Dutch for attacking them without provocation. This incident persuaded the Dutch to seek a peaceful accommodation with the Mohawks. The Dutch would for many years put continued pressure on the Mohawks and Mahicans to make peace, for the constant warfare was disrupting the normal trade relations of the Dutch and the Indians.

Europeans could make great fortunes in the Indian fur trade. A continuous supply of beaver skins had become as important to the economy of the Dutch, English, and French colonies as European trade goods had become to the Indians. The items most favored by the Indians were cloth, metal goods such as knives, hoes, kettles, and axes, and firearms and ammunition. Not only were they desirable, but they were becoming essential to the Indians, who were growing increasingly dependent upon their European trade partners.

The Mohawks continued to acquire European firearms from both the Dutch and English, despite an official Dutch prohibition against trading arms with them. This made the Mohawks formidable opponents against Indian enemies and against the French in Canada. The unity of the five tribes also strengthened the Iroquois in their dealings with the outside world. Their fortunate geographical location, along the great river systems and lakes, gave them a strategic military advantage. They could travel easily and quickly over the vast inland waterways they controlled, and they could intercept enemies, attack French and Indian villages, raid the fur-laden canoes of Huron and Algonquin fur traders on their way to barter with the French, and monopolize the fur trade with the Dutch and English along the Hudson River.

As economic motivation now became a strong factor in Indian warfare, the Iroquois were in a particularly fortunate position both militarily and diplomatically. They could make alliances with competing European colonial governments whenever it seemed to their advantage. Both the Dutch and the English sought and obtained Iroquois friendship and alliances.

The French, because of their alliances with the Hurons and the Algonquian-speaking Indians of Canada, were unable, despite occasional but earnest efforts, to achieve a permanent peace with the Iroquois Confederacy. The best the French could do was to protect the Iroquois religious converts their missionaries had made during brief periods of peace by moving them to Catholic Iroquois villages they had established in Canada.

The Iroquois quickly learned to adapt their military tactics to changing conditions of warfare. The wooden body armor that had been ample protection against stone weapons was ineffective against European firearms and the metal arrowheads acquired from the Europeans. They therefore abandoned their useless armor and changed their style of attack. Instead of the massed charges of armored warriors on the battlefield, which had been their favored practice, they adopted a more individualistic style of warfare in which warriors fired while concealed behind trees and rocks. Stealth, surprise, and ambush were the tactics at which the Iroquois became masters. They did continue, however, to use mass surprise attacks against enemy Indian villages, where they would terrorize and overwhelm their opponents by the sheer force of their numbers and the fury of their onslaught. A steady supply of firearms obtained in trade from the English and Dutch and the joint cooperation on the warpath of two or more of the Five Nations gave the Iroquois a strong advantage over their opponents.

Economic motives were not the sole reason for an increase in Indian warfare after the arrival of the Europeans. The newcomers had brought with them diseases against which the native Americans had no immunity and for which their healers knew no cures. Smallpox,

A French Canadian wearing Indian snowshoes. European artists relied on travelers' accounts to illustrate North American life.

measles, influenza, the common cold, lung infections, colic (abdominal cramps), and severe fevers were particularly deadly. Epidemics swept through Indian villages, drastically reducing their populations. The Iroquois were hit by a number of these devastating epidemics throughout the 17th century. For purposes of self-preservation, warfare to obtain captives for adoption became increasingly necessary for the people of the Five Nations.

THE IROQUOIS HOMELAND AND EUROPEAN TRADING CENTERS
LATE 16TH TO MID-17TH CENTURIES

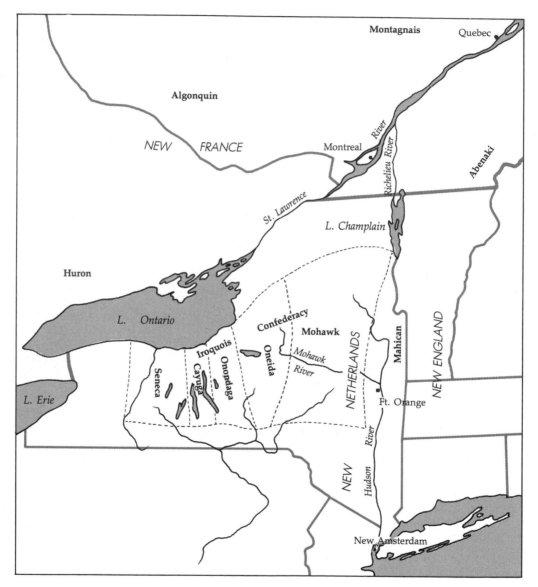

In the 1630s and 1640s, the Mohawks made efforts to conclude peace agreements with various opponents in order to wage war more successfully against others. By 1643, they had settled their previous differences with the Dutch and negotiated an important treaty with them. This alliance would be permanent and would prove mutually beneficial both economically and militarily. The Dutch gained strong allies, made even stronger by their increasing supply of Dutch firearms. The Mohawks achieved more control over

Champlain wampum belt. The five white circles against the background of purple shell beads symbolize the five nations of the Iroquois in the 18th century.

the fur trade, because commerce between the Dutch and the western tribes had to pass through their territory. Dutch friendship with the Mohawks also expanded to include the Iroquois tribes who lived to their west. When the English later conquered the colony of New Netherland and renamed it New York, they inherited and continued the Dutch alliance with the Iroquois.

After the Mohawks had secured Dutch friendship, they turned northward. They concluded a major peace treaty in 1645 with the French and their Huron and Algonquin allies. For the Mohawks, the peace was an opportunity to exchange prisoners and to hunt freely in the north country. The peace was also profitable for the French colonists, for it permitted the fur trade to flourish, uninterrupted by Mohawk attacks.

This tranquil situation lasted for nearly two years. When there seemed to be no more prisoners to exchange, and when peaceful hunting did not supply the Mohawks with enough furs for their insatiable trading needs, warfare broke out again. The Mohawks once more began raiding in Canada and encouraged the western tribes of the Iroquois Confederacy to attack the French and Hurons.

The Iroquois were on the verge of a new era of militancy that would take them to the peak of their power on the continent. The resulting conflict marked the start of one of the most bloody and devastating series of wars in American Indian history. ▲

A 19th-century Seneca men's headdress for special occasions from the Grand River Reservation. It is made from eagle and pheasant feathers and a leather cap with a perforation-decorated silver band.

THE EXPANSION OF IROQUOIS POWER

The short-lived peace made by the Mohawks with the French and their Indian allies did not include the other nations of the Iroquois Confederacy. The Senecas in particular continued their raids against the Wendots, or Hurons, as the Europeans called them. For the Oneidas, Onondagas, Cayugas, and Senecas, as with the Mohawks, warfare was increasingly motivated by economic considerations. The Hurons had access to a large beaver-hunting territory and also received in trade huge supplies of beaver pelts from hunting tribes living north and west of them. The Hurons' great success in the fur trade and their access to European trade goods made them the envy of the confederacy Iroquois. Warfare in the traditional style for prestige and revenge continued, but the economic motive now gave the wars an intensity they had previously lacked. Raids for plunder became of growing importance to the Iroquois tribes in the early 1640s. They began to devastate the Huron homeland, destroy villages,

kill or take prisoner large numbers of Hurons, and carry away great quantities of furs.

An army of more than 1,000 Seneca, Cayuga, and Onondaga warriors prepared to march against the Hurons in early 1647. Through vigorous peace efforts, the Hurons convinced the three central tribes of the Iroquois Confederacy—the Oneidas, Onondagas, and Cayugas—that a truce would be more profitable. These Iroquois and the Hurons exchanged prisoners and valuable gifts of wampum and enjoyed several months of peace. The Mohawks and Senecas, however, kept up the pressure of their raids against the Hurons.

In 1648, the Dutch in the New Netherland colony adopted an official government policy of selling guns directly to the Mohawks. Governor Peter Stuyvesant fully realized that the Mohawks' demand for firearms to improve their ability to hunt was only a pretext to secure guns to wage war more effectively. Nonetheless, he approved the sale of

Peter Stuyvesant, director-general of the colony of New Netherlands, 1646–64.

400 guns directly to these Mohawk friends. Any Mohawk attack on the French or their Indian allies would benefit the Dutch, who were rivals of the French in the fur trade.

Both failure and success in war came to the Iroquois in 1648. A large Mohawk war party that had attacked a Huron fur fleet near Montreal suffered a decisive defeat, but a Seneca penetration into the Huron homeland was mostly successful.

The large Seneca army attacked the fortified Huron village of Teanaostaiaé very early on the morning of July 3, 1648. The Jesuits had established a mission in the community of about 2,000 inhabitants. The Hurons were just leaving sunrise mass when the Senecas burst into town, setting fire to the longhouses, killing, and looting. The Hurons put up a spirited resistance that nearly succeeded, while their priest, Father Antoine Daniel, encouraged them and went through the village sprinkling the defenders, the sick, and the aged with holy water. When the tide of the battle started to turn against them, some Hurons began to flee; others gathered in the church seeking divine protection. Father Daniel urged them to flee also, and he strode out of the church to confront the enemy alone. The startled Senecas stared at him for a moment, then fired a volley of bullets and arrows at the courageous priest. They hacked his lifeless body to pieces in accordance with their custom of showing contempt for enemies and threw it back into the church, which had caught fire from the nearby burning longhouses. This brave confrontation by Father Daniel diverted the attention of the attackers long enough for most of the Hurons to escape.

The defeat was a serious blow to the Hurons. Seven hundred of them were either killed or taken prisoner and more than 1,000 were dispersed as refugees to other Huron villages. Teanaostaiaé was permanently abandoned. It was far too late in the season for the refugees to clear new fields and plant crops. The strain on the food resources of the villages that took in these unfortunates was thus enormous. The Hurons feared that the Iroquois would attack their other villages and destroy them as well. Huron morale was low.

Shortly after their victory over the Hurons, the Senecas entered into an alliance with the Mohawks for a joint campaign into Huron country. In the fall of 1648, an army of more than 1,000 Senecas and Mohawks left for the forested area north of Lake Ontario, where they lived and hunted undetected all winter. Their plan was to put themselves in an advantageous position from which to launch an attack on the Hurons when they least expected it. With the Iroquois were a number of Hurons who had been captured and adopted by the Senecas and Mohawks some years earlier. These adopted Huron war captives had become so completely integrated into Iroquois society that they now fought as loyal Iroquois warriors against their own people.

On the night of March 16, 1649, the Iroquois army silently approached the Huron village of Taenhatentaron and carefully assessed the situation. Though the village was stoutly stockaded and surrounded on three sides by ravines, it displayed a number of weaknesses to the enemy. Most of the inhabitants seemed to have departed several months earlier; only about 400 were still there. Furthermore, apparently because the winter was barely over, the inhabitants felt safe from attack and carelessly had not posted sentinels on the stockade watchtowers. The advantage lay with the Iroquois. They broke with their tradition of fighting only during the daytime and took advantage of the darkness for a surprise attack.

Quickly and quietly, the warriors cut through the stockade and poured into the village. In a one-sided battle the invaders soon captured the town, losing only 10 men in the action. They made a rich haul of booty and captives and turned the town into a fortified Iroquois outpost. Only three Huron men escaped to raise the alarm in the countryside.

Before the night was out, a detachment of Iroquois warriors proceeded toward the mission village of St. Louis. Warned by the Hurons who had escaped from Taenhatentaron, St. Louis had braced for the coming attack. The women and children had fled toward the larger mission village of Sainte-Marie, leaving behind 80 able-bodied warriors as well as those too sick or feeble to make the journey. The Huron defenders of St. Louis resisted fiercely, killing 30 of the enemy before being overcome. Only two warriors escaped to carry the warning to Sainte-Marie. The Iroquois killed the sick and elderly and set fire to the village. They took their captives, including two Jesuit priests, Father Jean de Brébeuf and Gabriel Lalemant, back to Taenhatentaron for torture.

News of the calamity spread rapidly from one Huron village to another. Warriors from distant Huron settlements flocked to Sainte-Marie to defend the village against the expected Iroquois onslaught. They did not have many hours to wait.

On March 17, the greater part of the Iroquois army moved toward Sainte-

The martyrdom of the Jesuit priests Jean de Brébeuf and Gabriel Lalemant. In 1649 the Iroquois attacked their mission village, slaughtering most of the Huron defenders and capturing the two Jesuits. Captives were either adopted or killed as a sacrifice.

Marie. The Hurons, who were scouting the countryside in anticipation of the attack, encountered about 200 warriors, the vanguard of the invading army. After a fierce seesaw battle, the Hurons finally drove the Iroquois back to St. Louis and recaptured the village.

When the main Iroquois army caught up with the Huron victors at St. Louis, they concentrated on the reconquest of the battered village instead of continuing their march to Sainte-Marie. The battle raged well into the night, with large loss of life on both sides. By the time the Iroquois had triumphed, there were only about 20 Huron defenders left, many of whom were already wounded.

The Iroquois invaders were disheartened by the large number of casualties they suffered and the heroic stand of the Hurons. Many began to withdraw and return homeward. The Iroquois leaders decided that the best policy would be to retreat, taking with them the captives on whom they had piled great amounts of booty.

Despite the fact that the Hurons had turned back the Iroquois invasion, panic now began to seize them. They had suffered through many years of incessant raids and two years of full-scale invasions. The previous year, 1648, Iroquois raids had disrupted their farming and had caused famine conditions in some villages. Fearing that this latest Iroquois invasion was the prelude to a long, terrifying season of warfare, the Hurons began to flee. Gathering their valuables and what little food they had, and burning their villages behind them, they deserted their country and took refuge with neighboring tribes.

Some went westward to the Tionontatehronons, or Mountain People, known to the Europeans as the Petuns, or Tobacco Nation. Others went southward to the Ontario peninsula to dwell with the Neutrals, or south of Lake Erie to the Erie Nation. All of these were Iroquois people but were not members of the Iroquois Confederacy. Other Huron refugees went to Gahoendoe, or Christian Island in Canada, where there

was a Jesuit mission. Nearly 8,000 took refuge on this small island in Georgian Bay, where they suffered famine and disease and died by the thousands. By the next year, only 500 remained alive at Gahoendoe, and these left to seek refuge with the French at Quebec.

The Iroquois had achieved their main purpose. The power of the Hurons was forever broken.

As long as there were still nations willing to show friendship to the refugee Hurons, however, the Iroquois felt that their borders were not safe. Also, the Iroquois wanted access to these nations' valuable hunting grounds. Accordingly, they wasted little time in attacking both the Tionontatehronons and the Neutrals.

In December 1649, an Iroquois war party entered Tionontatehronon territory. Warned of their coming by the Jesuits, warriors from the village of Etharita set out to meet them. Unfortunately, they missed the Iroquois, who had taken another route. Frustrated in their search, the warriors of Etharita returned to their village only to find it in ashes. Stunned by their failure to stop the enemy and by the severity of their loss, the warriors sat silently for half a day in mourning and shame.

By the spring of 1650, the surviving members of the Tionontatehronon Nation, along with their Huron companions, left their homeland and dispersed westward. This merged group, later known as Wyandots, wandered for years seeking a permanent home. By the mid-18th century, most Wyandots

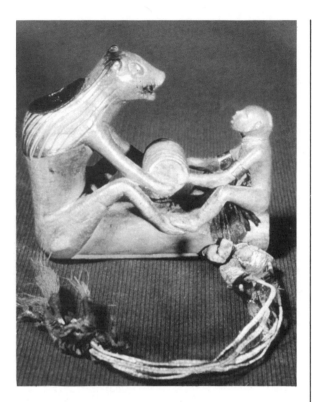

A Wyandot pipe bowl carved with a woman and a bear. After the Hurons and Petuns were nearly destroyed by Iroquois attackers, the survivors moved west and joined to form the Wyandots.

had settled in two areas: on the banks of the Detroit River and along the Sandusky River in Ohio country. Land pressures from non-Indian settlers later forced them to move, and in the 19th century they journeyed west, first to Kansas and then to Indian Territory (later to become the state of Oklahoma). Here a refugee group of Senecas offered them land along the Neosho River. Adversity would at last make friends of these former enemies.

In 1651, an army of Senecas invaded Neutral country. They were victorious at first, but the Neutrals finally defeated them and drove them back. The Iroquois returned a few months later, this time destroying the main Neutral town. They left with much booty and many captives. Now the hard-pressed Neutrals also abandoned their territory to the Iroquois and moved west to the vicinity of Saginaw Bay. From there they may eventually have moved south to the Ohio Valley. Wherever they went, these neutrals were henceforth lost to history.

After the total defeat of these Indian allies of the French, the four western nations of the Iroquois Confederacy sought to replace them as trading partners of the French. Irritated and greatly inconvenienced by Mohawk control over trade with the Dutch, these tribes were eager for a new source of commerce. The Senecas, Cayugas, Onondagas, and Oneidas therefore made peaceful overtures in 1653 to the French along the St. Lawrence. The French gladly assented, much relieved to be at peace with these troublesome Iroquois. The stable period that followed permitted a French Catholic mission and a trading post to be established at Onondaga.

Alarmed at being bypassed by their western associates, the Mohawks also concluded a peace with the French. During the next few months, however, they saw the Onondagas prospering and growing in both power and prestige as a result of their French alliance.

In a conference with the French at Quebec in 1654, the Mohawks made known their displeasure with the French attentions to the Onondagas. Their spokesman was a mixed-blood chief named Canaqueese, known to the Dutch as Jan Smits, son of a Dutch father and a Mohawk mother. Canaqueese described the political structure of the Extended Lodge to the French, informing them that the Mohawks were the Keepers of the Eastern Door and represented the proper entry to the confederacy. He berated the French for wrongfully entering the Lodge through the smoke hole (Onondaga), like a thief, rather than correctly through the front door. Despite this rebuke, the French continued to favor the Onondagas as trading partners.

Nothing could better illustrate the continuing tensions and rivalries that existed within the League itself than this speech of Canaqueese. Although the Five Nations were technically united, they were not always of the same mind.

The western Iroquois next turned their attention to the Erie Nation, who lived west of the Senecas and south of

Beaver, *sculpture of moose antler by Stan Hill, Mohawk, Six Nations Reserve, 1981. The beaver was an important Iroquois clan symbol long before the European demand for its fur. In addition, beavertail soup was a delicacy served on ceremonial occasions.*

Lake Erie. They were also an Iroquoian people but were never members of the League. Their presence in the Ohio Valley kept the Senecas from using that region as a hunting territory. Because the Erie also harbored Huron and Neutral refugees among them, the Senecas felt that their borders were unsafe. Furthermore, the Eries had angered the Onondagas by attacking and defeating an Onondaga war party in southern Ontario. Growing anti-Erie sentiment among the Iroquois soon resulted in a three-year war. By 1657, the Eries were totally defeated and dispersed; many were adopted by the Onondagas and Senecas. The remainder fled, maintaining their ethnic identity for a while but later disappearing as a separate identifiable group.

Within a decade, the Iroquois had completely smashed the great trading nations to the north and west of them, emerging as rulers over a vast domain. They had incorporated through adoption several thousand of their former rivals and thus considerably strengthened their confederacy. Had they been contented with their victories up to this point, and with exploiting the resources of the country they had just won, they might have enjoyed the rest of the century in peace. Instead they engaged in nearly 40 years of ruinous warfare from which, despite initial successes, they finally emerged in a much weakened state.

The Susquehannocks, a powerful Iroquoian tribe living south of the Iroquois Confederacy in Maryland and Pennsylvania, had a far-flung trading network, both with other Indian nations and with the nearby European colonists in Maryland, Delaware, and Virginia. They had been engaged in blood feuds with the confederacy Iroquois for well over a century. Flushed with their victory over the Hurons and their allies, the Iroquois, especially the Senecas and Mohawks, now turned against the Susquehannocks. They found these southerners no easy mark, for they were skilled warriors, living in stoutly fortified towns and well armed with European weapons, including cannons. It took 20 years of debilitating warfare for the Iroquois to conquer them.

Meanwhile, the peace that the French and Iroquois had made in 1653 was beginning to crumble. The Mohawks, jealous of the Onondagas' growing importance as a result of their French alliance, made plans to destroy the French mission at Onondaga. There was also resentment against the Jesuits among residents of Onondaga as a result of the diseases the French had inadvertently brought with them and against which the Indians had no immunity. Moreover, the new religion had begun to fragment the community. Followers of the Jesuits were no longer participating in the traditional ceremonies. This led some of the traditionalist Onondagas to plan an attack against the missionaries. Warned of the approaching danger by Iroquois friends, the Jesuits fled.

The Mohawks resumed hostilities along the Ottawa and St. Lawrence rivers in Canada, and Iroquois warriors attacked Indian allies of the French in the upper Great Lakes region. The French were rapidly becoming exasperated with the Iroquois.

In 1664, the English conquered New Netherland and renamed it New York.

These newcomers lost little time in negotiating treaties of friendship with the Indian allies of the Dutch. Fort Orange was renamed Albany and became the center of English treaty making with the Iroquois. The English alliance with the Five Nations would be of great significance to both sides during the various power struggles on the North American continent over the next 100 years. The Iroquois, with their favorable geographic location along the lakes and rivers of central and western New York, commanded the entire transportation network through their region as well as major routes to the west and south. They were thus in a strategically strong position commercially and militarily.

Also in 1664, the French made a firm decision to block continued Iroquois aggressions against them and their al-

lies. King Louis XIV of France sent the renowned Carnigan-Salières regiment to his American colony. These troops were under the command of the able veteran officer, the Marquis Prouville de Tracy. The king's instructions to the governor of New France were to initiate a military expedition against the Iroquois to "carry war even to their friends in order . . . to exterminate them."

News of the arrival of the French regiment spread rapidly throughout the country of the Extended Lodge. Representatives of the four western nations of the Iroquois Confederacy hastened to Canada to make peace with the French. The Mohawks stubbornly held out, complaining that the French had sent no official notice to them. De Tracy, determined that his troops

The wolf belt of the St. Regis Mohawk. The figures holding hands symbolize peace and friendship, which are being guarded by the wolves at both ends. Most surviving Iroquois belts were made in the 18th century.

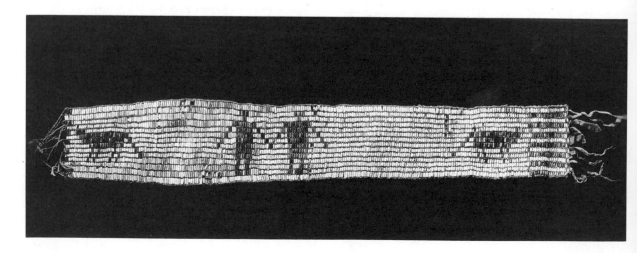

would be the official messengers to the recalcitrant Mohawks, launched an invasion of their territory in January 1666. Thwarted by the bitter winter weather and a Mohawk ambush, the French soon returned to Canada. They had, however, made their point, and the Mohawks asked to be included in the peace.

De Tracy soon claimed that the Mohawks were not abiding by the terms of the peace and so launched another invasion against them in the fall of 1666. This time he was successful. The French troops burned a hastily abandoned Mohawk village and destroyed all the crops and stored food supplies. Obviously the French did not intend to melt away before the Iroquois as the Hurons, the Neutrals, and others had done.

From then on, when peace treaties failed to secure the desired results, the French would resort to destructive military invasions of Iroquois country. The Five Nations now had a determined and formidable foe to face—a foe that would no longer remain quiet while the Five Nations attacked its Indian allies and undermined France's economic and political interests on the North American continent. ▲

Joseph Brant, painted by Gilbert Stuart in 1786. The Mohawk leader whose Indian name was Thayendanegea fought against the Americans in the Revolutionary War.

WARFARE
AND
DIPLOMACY

During their brief interlude of peace with the Iroquois, the French missionaries had been remarkably successful in making converts. In 1667 and 1668, a small group of Oneidas established themselves along the St. Lawrence River, near the French settlement of Montreal. These Oneidas became the nucleus of a rapidly growing village of Catholic Iroquois. Onondagas, Hurons, and especially Mohawks swelled the population of the village, which took the name Caughnawaga (At the Rapids).

The Caughnawagas became firm allies of the French, even joining with them in military expeditions against the Iroquois in their old homeland south of Lake Ontario. Throughout the century of conflict between the French and English for predominance in North America, the Caughnawagas continued to support the French.

The Iroquois attacks on the tribes of the western Great Lakes region in the late 17th century gradually merged with the European wars between the French and the English that had spilled over to the North American continent. The French intervention against the Iroquois in support of their own Indian allies would prove to be a serious obstacle to Iroquois ambitions.

The Iroquois did gain, at least in the short run, from their alliance with the English. When Edmund Andros became governor of the colony of New York in 1674, he proceeded immediately to renew and strengthen English alliances with all the Algonquian and Iroquois groups within New York's borders. In the earliest Dutch period, the Indians and Dutch had used the metaphor of "chains" to describe their alliances: "We are brothers and are joined together by chains." The implication was that nothing could break this "Covenant Chain" and disrupt the friendship. Governor Andros expanded this Covenant Chain tradition to attach the Iroquois more firmly to the English and to promote the interests of his New York colony. He forbade other English colonies to make any treaties with New York's Indian tribes unless sponsored by the New York government. In 1667, he permitted delegates from Maryland and Virginia to come to Albany, New York, to conduct peace negotiations with the Five Nations, whose warriors had recently been attacking the Indian tribes in those two colonies to the south. As a result of these negotiations, the Five Nations took Maryland and Virginia into the Covenant Chain. This enhanced the prestige and power of the colony of New York, securing English friendship for the Iroquois. It also enhanced the power of their confederacy by enabling them to incorporate other formerly hostile Indian tribes into the Extended Lodge.

The Covenant Chain would be manipulated by both the Five Nations and the English to increase their advantage over their opponents. The English now had the friendship of the most powerful Indian confederacy on the continent. The Iroquois, for their part, had made a valuable military and economic alliance with the aggressive English and had secured their borders to the east and south. To the north and west, however, were the French and their Indian allies and trading partners. In these regions, the Iroquois could feel no security except through warfare and conquest.

French copies of Iroquois drawings, 17th century. The top two rows show clan symbols. Third row center: a hunter killed three deer. Bottom left: a French sketch of warriors returning with scalps and a prisoner. Bottom center: a war council of the bear and beaver clans.

Beginning in 1680, the Iroquois carried on a devastating series of wars against these western Indians. The fur trade had become as important to the Iroquois as it was to the Europeans, and they determined to open new areas of supply. In one campaign after another they attacked the Illinois and Miami Indians of the Ohio and Illinois region, destroying their villages and killing or capturing huge numbers from each tribe. They alternately threatened and cajoled the Ottawa Indians north of the Great Lakes, who supplied the French with two-thirds of their furs. The French had a string of forts in the Illinois and upper Great Lakes regions. Seeing their position dangerously threatened by repeated Iroquois aggressions, they decided to intervene.

In June of 1687, Jacques-René de Brisay Denonville, the governor of New France, led an invading force of more than 2,000 French and Indians against the Senecas, destroying their villages, their standing crops, and their stored grain. The next year, the Cayugas, Onondagas, and Oneidas traveled to Montreal to negotiate a treaty with Denonville. The peace would not last long. Less than two years later, King William's War (1689–97) broke out between France and England. The Iroquois seized the opportunity and once more went on the offensive against the French, attacking the settlement of Lachine, not far from Montreal.

The French continually retaliated against the English and their Iroquois allies during the course of the war. In

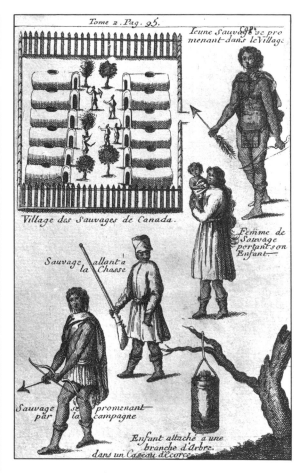

An illustration from an 18th-century French book recounting a "dialogue between baron de Lahontan and an American savage." The word "sauvage" referred to a person who lived intimately with nature. This was later considered an ideal state for humanity.

February 1690, the new governor of New France, Louis de Buade de Frontenac, with a force of 210 French troops and Caughnawaga Indian allies, attacked and destroyed the English village of Schenectady northwest of Albany. Three years later, in 1693,

Frontenac surprised and destroyed the three Mohawk villages and took 300 captives. In July 1696, with 2,200 French and Indian troops, he successfully attacked the Oneidas and again the Onondagas.

In the western Great Lakes region, the Ojibwas led a coalition of Ottawas and Potawatomis known as the Council of the Three Fires. The warriors of the Three Fires hammered the Iroquois relentlessly and in three fierce battles in 1696 drove them out of the Ontario peninsula and claimed it as their own.

The Iroquois suffered an enormous number of casualties in these western wars. Instead of achieving their purpose, they who had once been the invincible conquerors of a vast territory were now themselves defeated. In the last decade of the 17th century alone they had lost at least 1,600 and perhaps as many as 2,000 of their own people. They had seen their homeland invaded and destroyed again and again by the French and their Indian allies. Now their western landholdings were being destroyed as well.

The Iroquois decided that the time had come for a new strategy. In early 1700, they sent out peace feelers to Governor Louis-Hector de Callière of New France. The governor responded favorably but insisted that the Indian allies of the French also be included in the peace. Both sides promised to return their prisoners and the Iroquois further requested the resumption of trade with the French and access to their smiths, who could repair their guns and tools.

They reminded the governor that they were making peace with him despite English disapproval and so asked for his protection should the English try to punish them. Governor Callière gladly agreed to all of the Iroquois requests. Both sides set August 1701 as the date for a great gathering at Montreal when the final treaty would be approved by all the warring parties.

The chief author of this new peace policy was the Onondaga statesman Teganissorens, pronounced by the English as Decanesora. He was the greatest orator of his day. One New Yorker who was acquainted with him likened him to the great Roman statesman Cicero. A man of abundant wisdom and ability and a true patriot, Teganissorens realized that the Iroquois' best interests lay in maintaining neutrality between the French and the English, not letting either European nation gain a predominance of power. The most important task for the Iroquois was now to preserve their own territory and their independence.

The new peace policy brought social and economic benefits to the Iroquois. Freed from danger from the north and west, they could now hunt and even settle in the Ohio region without fear of attack. They had granted the western Great Lakes Indians the right to travel through their territory to trade with them and with the English. The Iroquois profited greatly from this commerce, because they received additional furs from these western Indians in exchange for the goods and food they

supplied to the journeyers. The Iroquois could also trade with the French at Fort Frontenac on the northeastern shore of Lake Ontario, as well as at the new small trading post opened by the French at Irondequoit on the south shore of Lake Ontario.

When the French established a trading post at Niagara and a few years later strengthened it by building a large stone fort, the Iroquois became alarmed at such a formidable military presence in their territory. They therefore permitted the British to build a fort at the

A WOMAN
TO BE VENERATED

Among the Mohawks who moved to Caughnawaga in 1667 was a young woman, Tekakwitha, who was living in the longhouse of her uncle. She had been born in 1656. Her mother, a Christian Algonquin, had been captured by a band of Mohawks at Three Rivers, near Quebec, and married a Mohawk chief, which saved her from death or slavery. When Tekakwitha was about four years old, her parents and younger brother died in a smallpox epidemic. She alone of her family recovered, her eyesight permanently damaged and her skin pockmarked. She was adopted and cared for by her father's brother, a village chief, and so she learned the ways of her Mohawk people.

French attacks in 1666 destroyed Tekakwitha's village. The surviving Mohawks moved farther west, joining other refugee Iroquois at Caughnawaga, near Montreal, and finally making peace with the French. Several Jesuit missionaries came to Caughnawaga in 1667, and stayed for three days in Tekakwitha's uncle's longhouse. Two years later, construction began on St. Peter's Chapel in the village. When Tekakwitha was 19 years old, she asked the Jesuits to give her instruction in the Catholic faith. She resisted the efforts of her relatives to arrange a marriage for her in the Indian way. On Easter Sunday in 1676, she was baptized as Catherine (Katherine in English, Kateri in the Mohawk language).

Many of the Mohawks in the village were still traditional, and they harassed those who, like Kateri, attempted to observe the Christian faith. Stones were thrown at her when she refused to go to work in the cornfields on Sundays. She decided to take the earliest opportunity to leave Caughnawaga for the St. Francis mission south of the St. Lawrence River in Canada, at Sault St. Louis. Her chance came in late 1677 when three Christian Indians from St. Francis, one of them a relative of hers, came to visit Caughnawaga. Her uncle was away at the time and unable to prevent her departure.

Tekakwitha took her first communion at the mission before Christmas that same year. A few months later she was accepted into the Society of the Holy Family and took a vow never to marry. Despite her physical disabilities and daily attendance at services, she continued to carry out her traditional Indian work obligations when they did not interfere with her religious observances.

Her health had been poor since childhood, and in early 1680 she became quite ill. She died a few months later, on April 17, only 24 years of age. The priest who attended her reported to all his wonder at seeing her pockmarked face become clear and beautiful.

Kateri Tekakwitha immediately became the subject of prayer and reverence. French as well as Indian Christians visited her grave with personal prayers, and their devotions were often rewarded. Two Jesuits published works about her before the end of the 17th century. In the early 20th century, her followers were successful in getting the Vatican to take the first of the steps that could lead to sainthood for Kateri. In 1932 she was declared venerable. An investigation was authorized into the "Cause of Catherine Tekakwitha," and documents on her behalf were gathered (published in English in 1940 by Fordham University Press in New York City). Three hundred years after her death, on June 22, 1980, she was accorded the second step leading to sainthood and was beatified. Her advocates continue to visit the National Shrine of North American Martyrs in Auriesville, New York, near the village in which Kateri was born and spent most of her life, as well as the Saint Francis Xavier Mission in Caughnawaga and Sault St. Louis near Montreal in Canada, where she died. Only the final step of canonization remains to make Kateri Tekakwitha the first American Indian to become a saint.

There are several statues of Kateri Tekakwitha at the Shrine of Our Lady of Martyrs, Auriesville, New York, near where she was born in 1656.

mouth of the Oswego River and Lake Ontario. The French instantly recognized the Iroquois strategy of balancing one European nation against another.

For most of the next half century, the Iroquois lapsed only occasionally from their policy of neutrality. This policy was often under great strain, however, for pro-French and pro-English factions had developed within each tribe of the Five Nations. The strongest French advocates were among the Senecas and Onondagas. The English had more supporters among the Mohawks, who lived closer to Albany and the English settlements. During the various phases of Queen Anne's War (1702–13), King George's War (1744–48), and the French and Indian War (1754–63), the English were always able to rouse a number of Iroquois warriors to accompany their expeditions against the French. Despite these violations of the peace by individual warriors, the neutrality policy continued until the middle of the 18th century. The long period of peace enabled the Iroquois to rebuild their communities, increase their population, and expand their trade.

The English as well as the French recognized the political importance of establishing religious missions among the Indians they wished to attach to their cause. The Jesuits had been depleting the population of Iroquois country for years by luring large numbers of converts to their Catholic villages at Caughnawaga, near Montreal, and Oswegatchie (present-day Ogdensburg, New York). The former village was composed mostly of Mohawks and the latter mostly of Onondagas and Cayugas. Around 1750, a group of Caughnawagas settled farther up the St. Lawrence River, where the French established a mission named St. Regis. Jesuit missionaries continued to be active among the Iroquois who remained in their homeland, where a number of converts, loyal both to their new faith and to the French who had converted them and who continued to show them favors, still lived.

The English were quick to learn the lesson and to take an interest in ministering to the Iroquois. The earliest efforts of English missionaries among the Mohawks, however, met with little response.

For many years, Dutch Reformed pastors who lived in or near Albany had also ministered to their Mahican and Mohawk neighbors and had made a number of converts. One young man, destined in later years to be a great leader among his people, was Theyanoguin, a Mahican who had been adopted by the Mohawks and who had become a chief. He took an interest in Christianity and was converted to the Protestant faith by the Dutch pastor Godfrey Dellius. The Dutch and English knew him as Hendrick or, because of his chiefly status, King Hendrick. Enthusiastic about his new faith, Hendrick began to preach among the Mohawks.

In 1710, during Queen Anne's War, English officials at Albany were disturbed about their government's lack of interest in Indian affairs. They therefore

The four chiefs who went to London were painted there in 1710. Left: *Chief Hendrick, with the wolf, his clan symbol, at lower left.* Right: *Sa Ga Yeath Qua Pieth Tow, Mohawk of the bear clan. Engravings made from these paintings were widely distributed in the colonies.*

decided to send a delegation to England to emphasize the importance of holding on to Indian support. Colonel Francis Nicholson and Peter Schuyler took with them four chiefs: Hendrick, two other Mohawks, and a Mahican. Schuyler, a former mayor of Albany and a wealthy fur trader, had many years' experience in negotiating with Indians on behalf of the city of Albany and the colony of New York. He was held in particularly high regard by the Iroquois, who had come to consider him their special intermediary with the colonial government.

In London, the Indians were a sensation. They were entertained everywhere, had their portraits painted, and were presented at court. The "Four Kings," as they were known in England, asked Queen Anne to send help to combat the French and to provide Church of England missionaries for the Indian villages. The queen assented and became the patron of the Mohawk mission.

The Anglican missionary organization, the Society for Propagating the Gospel, had increased success in the years that followed in converting

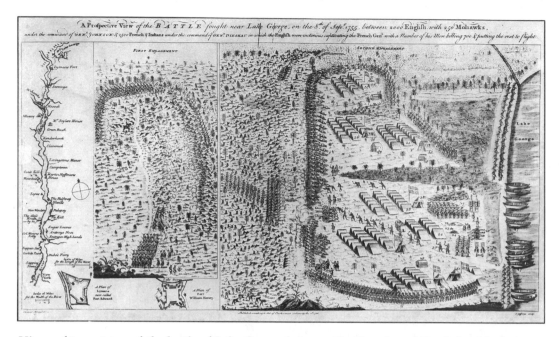

Views of two stages of the battle of Lake George between the French and English with their respective Indian allies. At left is the Hudson River from New York City to Lake George.

the Mohawks to the Anglican faith. The missionaries also devised a system of writing the Mohawk language, provided schooling for young Mohawks, and translated religious literature into Mohawk. Hendrick became an Anglican lay preacher and the strongest supporter of the missionaries. By the 1740s, most Mohawks were at least nominal Protestant Christians and were firm friends of the English.

So loyal were the Mohawks that in later years the English would often refer to them as "the faithful Mohawks." One of the most faithful was Chief Hendrick. In 1755, when he was well past 70 years of age, he would put himself at the head of 300 warriors and join the

English in an expedition against the French. At a battle near Lake George in the Adirondacks, the English and Mohawks would defeat the invading French army, but the courageous Hendrick would lose his life.

But in the early 18th century, as a result of the peace settlement of 1701 following their defeats in the 1690s, the Iroquois sought ways to regain power. Military means were closed to them, so they turned to political efforts. A part of their strategy was to cooperate with the government of Pennsylvania and to assert the authority of the Iroquois Confederacy over the Indian tribes of that region. These Pennsylvania tribes were the Lenni Lenape (Delaware), Shawnees, Conestogas (the remnant of the Susquehannocks), and Conoys (Piscataways). Pennsylvania officials saw an advantage in developing a special friendship with the Iroquois, because the confederacy could help control the tribes within their borders. They were particularly concerned that the Shawnees had become too friendly with the French. This "Pennsylvania policy" was thus mutually beneficial to Pennsylvania and the Iroquois.

After the Iroquois had agreed not to fight against France's Indian allies in the west, they turned their hostilities against the Indians of the south. In a long series of wars lasting more than 50 years, mainly against the Catawbas and the Cherokees in the Carolinas and Georgia, the Iroquois gained both prestige and captives. The English repeatedly tried to get the Iroquois to stop these attacks on their Indian allies, but the League persisted. They had everything to gain and nothing to lose. The French and their western Indian allies benefited by these wars, for the French had colonial interests in the south and were delighted to see English allies being destroyed. Once more the Iroquois were emerging as a force to be reckoned with.

The Iroquois' wars in the south brought them in touch with the problems of the Tuscarora tribe in North Carolina. The Tuscaroras were an Iroquois group that had migrated south before the formation of the confederacy but who still remembered their kinship with the northern tribes. Their non-Indian neighbors in North Carolina had for many years been encroaching upon their lands and kidnapping their children to sell into slavery. Pressed beyond their endurance, the Tuscaroras declared war on the colonists. The North Carolinians received the military support of colonists and various Indian allies, including the Catawbas, the Cherokees, and the Yamasees, from South Carolina. The Tuscaroras, defeated in the 1711–13 wars, migrated north to Pennsylvania and New York to take refuge in the Extended Lodge. The Oneidas adopted them and they became the sixth tribe of the League. The Five Nations, now strengthened and enlarged, would from this time on be known as the Six Nations.

The Iroquois were able to play their neutrality game between the French and English only until the end of the French and Indian War (1754–63). After that, the victorious English deprived France of its American colonies and emerged as the major power on the East Coast, in Canada, and in the Ohio region. Even during that war, the Iroquois had not been completely neutral, nor were they united in taking sides. The Mohawks had generally supported the English and the Senecas had fought with the pro-French Indians. Now the English occupied former French forts in Canada and the West, and they were far less accommodating to the Indians than the French had been. They had no need to be overly generous to the Indians, who could no longer ally themselves with the French.

Molly Brant, leader of the Iroquois women, commemorated on a 1986 Canadian stamp.

Indian resentment against the English flared up in a brief war known as Pontiac's Conspiracy (1763–64), after the Ottawa war leader who organized this rebellion. The Senecas took an enthusiastic part in this uprising, attempting to drive the British out of the West. The war failed in its objective and was soon over.

Sir William Johnson, the superintendent of Indian affairs for the northern department of Britain's American colonies, scolded the Senecas for their part in the war. As punishment, he forced them to cede some of their territory to the Crown.

Johnson had come to America from Ireland in 1738 to manage the Mohawk Valley estate of his absentee uncle, Admiral Peter Warren. With financial help from Warren, Johnson acquired more and more land in that area, employing white servants and black slaves to work his property. He also went into business, importing goods from England to exchange for Iroquois furs. His farming and trading enterprises both prospered. He had been adopted by the Mohawks and was thoroughly acquainted with their culture. A Mohawk woman, Mary Brant (or Molly Brant, as she was better known), served as his housekeeper and his wife. Although he never legally married her, he treated her with great respect and affection. He raised all his children by her in the style becoming the sons and daughters of an English country gentleman. His wealth and community standing, combined with his good relationship with the Iroquois, led to the government appointment to manage Indian affairs, a post in which he served for years.

In the years following Pontiac's War, when Sir William Johnson was urging the Six Nations to hold fast to the Covenant Chain, trouble was brewing in the colonies. The settlers were becoming rebellious and protesting against British taxes. Sir William was concerned that the growing quarrel between the colonists and the Crown might disrupt the British-Indian alliances. He was particularly worried about the missionary to the Oneidas, Samuel Kirkland, who also worked among the Tuscaroras. Kirkland was not a member of the Church of England but a New England Puritan. He sided with the colonists, not with their British government. Johnson tried to remove Kirkland but found that Oneida members of his church stood solidly behind their missionary.

Sir William died suddenly in 1774, during a treaty council with the Iroquois. He was succeeded in his office by his nephew, Colonel Guy Johnson. It was now Guy Johnson's task to hold the Iroquois loyal to the Crown as the colonists headed toward separation from Great Britain.

The American Revolution had a tragic impact on the Six Nations. The neutrality they had sought to maintain between contending parties broke down under pressures from the British and the colonials. The warfare that erupted in the country surrounding the Six Nations Confederacy eventually drew them all into the conflict, and they were not all of the same mind. Two of the most active Mohawk supporters of the Crown were Molly Brant and her younger brother Joseph, an energetic war chief. Meanwhile, the Oneidas had begun to enlist in the militia units being formed in towns in the Mohawk River Valley to fight against the Loyalists, who sided with the British.

In previous wars, when the Iroquois nations had divergent allegiances, they had been able to fight their respective opponents without fighting one another. The American Revolution would change all that. The confederacy council could not control the warriors in each nation. Each nation therefore chose sides for itself. The Oneidas and Tus-

"Public Testimonial . . . of . . . Esteem & Approbation" given by Sir William Johnson to Iroquois for "Attachment to his Britanic Majesty's Interests, and Zeal for his Service."

caroras chose the new American union. The Mohawks, Onondagas, Cayugas, and Senecas chose the king. The hostilities that raged through their own country and the surrounding non-Indian settlements meant that on more than one occasion, Iroquois was fighting Iroquois.

So destructive were the raids of the pro-British Iroquois and Loyalists that the government of New York appealed to the Continental Congress for help. In 1779, General George Washington authorized an invasion of Iroquois country. The officer in charge of the expedition was Major General John Sul-

The Seneca chief Cornplanter, in an oil painting done in New York in 1796

livan. A companion army under Brigadier General James Clinton joined Sullivan. In the fall, the two armies set off on what was to be the successful destruction of all the hostile Indian villages east of the Genesee River.

The Sullivan-Clinton campaign pushed the Loyalist Iroquois back to Fort Niagara. Here the British army and Indian Department were forced to protect and provide for the starving and homeless Indians throughout the severe winter that followed.

The American invasion did not defeat the Iroquois but merely increased their desire for revenge. The following spring, they came back with even more ferocity. Joseph Brant, although not the leading warrior of the confederacy, be-

came particularly active throughout the war. He led a raiding party that burned the Oneida and Tuscarora villages in retaliation for their support of the Americans.

The most distinguished warrior of the League was Kayengkwaahton, or "Old Smoke," of the Senecas. Now elderly but still vigorous, he usually had to ride a horse on long marches in order to keep up with the younger warriors. The young Cornplanter, another Seneca, also held one of the leading positions as war chief of the confederacy.

The British completely ignored their Indian allies when they signed the Treaty of Paris, which ended the war with the United States in 1783. The Iroquois were horrified and incensed at what they considered a betrayal of their loyal services. British officers still in North America were also embarrassed by their government's neglect of the Indians whom, after all, they had enticed into the war. General Frederick Haldimand, commander of the British forces in Canada, pressured his government to grant land to the Loyalist Iroquois so they would not be left to the revenge of the victors.

The British government gave its approval and Haldimand bought a large tract of land from the Mississauga Indians along the Grand River on the Ontario peninsula. He presented it to the Mohawks and the other Loyalist Iroquois—"His Majesty's faithful Allies," as the general called them. Most of the Loyalist Iroquois who wished to migrate followed Joseph Brant to Grand

The silver medal given by Sir William Johnson to the western Iroquois in 1766. On one side is King George III; on the reverse, an Englishman and Indian with peace pipe shaking hands. The Iroquois eagle is at the top.

River. Another group of Mohawks, under John Deserontyon, settled north of the Bay of Quinté, with Haldimand's help.

On the Grand River Reservation, there were members of all the Six Nations. It is known today as the Six Nations Reserve. Most Senecas, however, elected to remain in their own country rather than emigrate to Canada.

After centuries of conquest and domination, the Extended Lodge was now disrupted and its nations dispersed. The Iroquois were beginning a new phase in their history: the reservation period. ▲

"A Class of Mohawk Children" at the Grand River school appeared in A Primer for the Use of the Mohawk Children, *published in London in 1786. Males, including the teacher, wear European-style clothing along with the traditional scalplock and earrings.*

DECLINE
AND
REVIVAL

Because many pro-British Iroquois moved to the Grand River Reservation in Canada after the American Revolution, the geographic organization of the Extended Lodge was disrupted. The Mohawks were no longer actually Keepers of the Eastern Door, for they had all abandoned their former home territory along the Mohawk River. The only Mohawk group still remaining in New York was the St. Regis settlement in the far north along the St. Lawrence River. The people here were Catholics who had earlier moved to a Jesuit community and were not members of the confederacy. Many Onondagas and Cayugas had gone westward to live among the Senecas at Buffalo Creek (site of the present-day city of Buffalo).

Despite the division and disruption of the League, the leaders on both sides of the border attempted to mend the breach and reorganize the confederacy. They moved their council fire from its ancient seat at Onondaga to Buffalo Creek, which was now their most cen-

tral location. The wampum of the confederacy was also transferred to Buffalo Creek.

For a number of years, this arrangement worked and the confederacy continued to function. Iroquois from all the villages would travel to Buffalo Creek for the important confederacy council meetings and diplomatic transactions. Only later did the confederacy become divided by the United States-Canadian border.

After the end of the Revolution and the signing of the peace treaty between the United States and Great Britain, the Continental Congress appointed commissioners to make peace with the four hostile Iroquois nations—the Mohawks, Onondagas, Cayugas, and Senecas. The commissioners traveled with a military guard to Fort Stanwix, near Oneida Lake. The Treaty of Fort Stanwix, signed on October 22, 1784, was an imposed peace, not a peace between equals. The Loyalist Iroquois claimed that they had not been defeated

Mohawk village on the Grand River, painted in watercolors on bark in 1793. The large building at the left may have belonged to Joseph Brant; the church is at the right.

in battle by the United States. But now that they lacked British military support, they were unable to defend their sovereignty or their land rights. From the Indians' point of view, the British had not only deserted them but had turned their whole country over to the United States by the terms of the Treaty of Paris. Intimidated by the presence of soldiers and the aggressive behavior and demands of the U.S. commissioners, the Iroquois had no alternative but to agree to the terms being imposed on them.

The Treaty of Fort Stanwix brought peace to the four hostile tribes and assured the two faithful tribes, the Onei-

das and Tuscaroras, of continued peaceful possession of their land. The commissioners took six delegates from the hostile tribes as hostages to assure the safe return of war prisoners still held by those tribes. The treaty set a boundary defining the limits of the Iroquois country. The new limits deprived them of much Seneca land in western New York and Pennsylvania and all the Ohio lands.

When the commissioners from the Continental Congress had concluded their treaty with the browbeaten Iroquois, commissioners from Pennsylvania stepped forward to negotiate a large land grant on behalf of their own state.

As payment, they offered the Indians $4,000 worth of goods, telling them that the land already belonged to Pennsylvania by the terms of the peace treaty with Great Britain. Confused and demoralized, the Iroquois delegates nonetheless did manage to negotiate another $1,000 worth of goods from the Pennsylvania delegates before finally agreeing. On October 23, 1784, they signed away a large tract of land in northwestern Pennsylvania.

Greatly angered by the loss of land agreed to by their delegates, the Six Nations council meeting at Buffalo Creek refused to ratify the Treaty of Fort Stanwix and even offered to return the gifts given to the delegates. Their protest was fruitless. As far as the United States government was concerned, the treaty was valid, whether the whole confederated Six Nations in council approved or not. The tactic of conquest by treaty would be used continually in the future in United States-Indian relations.

Those Iroquois who had gone to Canada had other difficulties. The tract of land along the Grand River was large but not as vast as the territory the Mohawks and their friends had left in their own country. Joseph Brant, or Thayendanegea, who emerged as the outstanding leader of the Six Nations Reserve, as their homeland was called in Canada, saw that there was too little land to support a hunting economy but more than could be farmed by the women in the present population. Most of the Indian men refused to take up farming because it was traditionally the

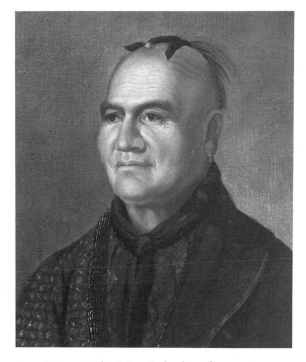

Joseph Brant, the Iroquois leader who went to the Six Nations Reserve in Canada after the Revolution, in an 1806 painting.

women's occupation. Brant saw that with hunting now restricted because of the smaller land base, farmers would have to raise substantial herds of domestic animals to provide meat. In order to put greater acreage into production than could be done with hand tools, the Indians would also have to use horse-drawn plows and harrows in breaking up and cultivating the ground. The effective use of these heavy implements called for greater physical strength than most women had.

Brant devised a plan to help his people make the transition to reservation living. He firmly believed that it would be necessary for the men to change their attitudes and adopt the non-Indians' style of farming to provide enough food for the whole population. To encourage the Indian men to become farmers, Brant proposed and other Iroquois leaders agreed to lease or sell parcels of their reservation to friendly non-Indian farmers. Brant had the support of the leading chief at Grand River, Henry Tekarihoga, sachem of the Turtle clan, who was Brant's wife's brother. Numbers of nearby whites, many of whom had fought beside the Indians in the recent war, gained grants on the Six Nations Reserve. And gradually, Indian men did begin to farm. Brant's program was thus successful, but only partially so, for it caused ongoing disputes.

British officials in Canada were determined that the Iroquois should not sell or lease any of their land to outsiders. It was meant for Indians only. Officials constantly warned Brant that the king's allies (the Iroquois) should not have the king's subjects (the English) as tenants. For years Brant conducted a running feud with the government representatives, insisting that the Indians should be able to do whatever they wanted with their own land.

In the end Brant had his way, but the results were not always what he and his supporters had wished. The property deeds were often so poorly drawn and the agreements so negligently enforced that the Six Nations Council frequently did not receive its lease money. Eventually, huge parcels of reservation land passed out of the Indians' control. More than 350,000 acres of reservation land were lost as a result of Brant's program.

His policy also led to factionalism on the Six Nations Reserve. Some people were bitterly opposed to granting any of their land to the whites. Many began to gossip that Brant was corrupt and was pocketing the lease money himself—a charge that was completely untrue.

The ultimate failure of the land-grant policy to provide the tribe with income and the great loss of reservation territory were not the result of corruption on the part of any member of the Six Nations Council. These problems stemmed from the Indians' lack of knowledge of the complexities of English real estate law and lack of experience as landlords and real estate entrepreneurs. To be successful in any enterprise involving land as a commodity and whites as purchasers or tenants, they would have had to know a great deal—how to survey lands, write deeds, keep records, collect rents and mortgage payments, and wisely invest the money received. They would also have had to know how to bring lawsuits against those who were delinquent in payments, hire competent and honest lawyers, carry out foreclosure proceedings, as well as find money to pay for lawyers and long-drawn-out legal maneuvers. Real estate was a business in which the Iroquois were at a decided

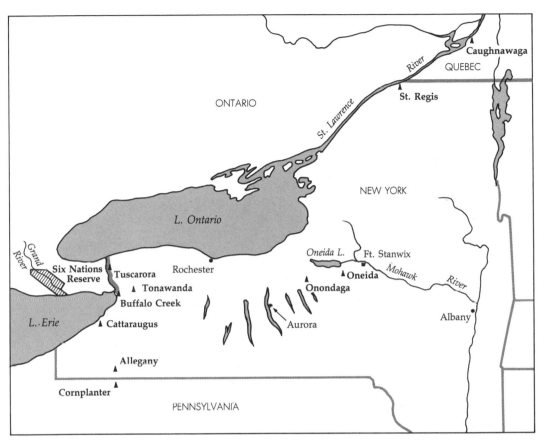

disadvantage. Even the non-Indian trustees later chosen to handle the Six Nations' finances made serious blunders and invested the Six Nations' income in a canal-building enterprise that failed dismally.

Long after Brant's death, non-Indians continued to be persistent trespassers on the reservation and to pressure the Indians to sell more land to them. In response to government concern that the reservation would soon dwindle away to nothing, the chiefs in 1841 voluntarily surrendered most of their remaining land to the Crown. They retained a smaller reserve that could be more easily managed and that would be forever guaranteed to them. The government officials then proceeded to evict the non-Indian squatters—illegal settlers—from the reserve. This was not easy but was eventually successful.

The confederacy Iroquois on the American side of the border did little better than the community in Canada in preserving their lands. The treaty of Fort Stanwix of 1784 had promised the Iroquois rights to peaceful occupation of their territory, then comprising most

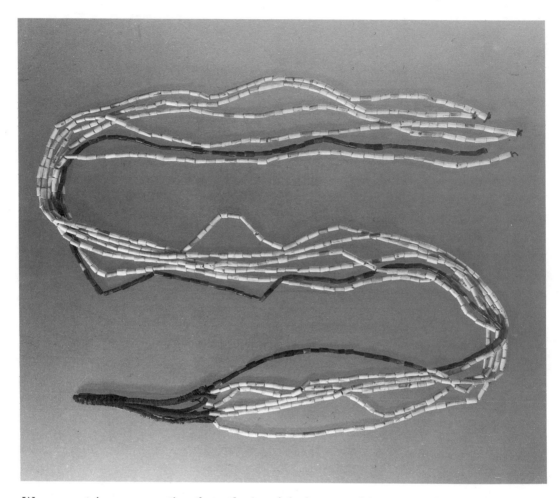

Wampum strings representing the authority of the league and its council, held by the speaker or firekeeper when opening and closing council meetings. The white strings represent the original five nations; the purple string represents peoples later adopted into the League. Wampum beads are made from a type of shell that is found only along the Atlantic coast of North America. The Iroquois got their shell beads in trade from the Indians of Long Island. In the 17th century the Dutch encouraged the use of wampum as a medium of exchange in the fur trade, and they set the value of the purple beads at two times that of the white beads.

of central and western New York. But by 1800, all that remained of that huge territory were a few small reservations. New York State officials, under the leadership of Governor George Clinton, relentlessly pressured the Iroquois to sell out. These officials planned to confine Indians to a few small villages in order to acquire the rest of their land, which they would sell to non-Indians. .

First the state officials and then agents of private land companies independently made treaties with the Iroquois tribes, successfully whittling away the Indians' domain. The directors of the land companies in particular anticipated huge profits from the sale of this vast territory to settlers. State officials wanted to populate western New York with non-Indians, who would carve out farms from the forest, build villages and cities, and thus strengthen the state politically and economically. In the process, the Iroquois lost out. The Oneida reservation was reduced to a few acres. The Cayugas sold all their land and went to live at Buffalo Creek with the Senecas. The Onondagas and Senecas also saw their land holdings drastically shrink.

Voluntarily, the Iroquois sold most of their land after 1784. They were strongly pressured but were not actually physically coerced as they had been at Fort Stanwix.

For more than a century, the practice of selling land had been familiar to many Iroquois. The offer of large quantities of gifts, including hoes, kettles, axes, domestic animals, cloth, firearms, gunpowder, and other useful items, and the further promise of additional money payments were tempting to Indians who had become dependent upon manufactured items from Europe that made life easier for them. Bribes and lifetime pensions were also sometimes offered to certain leading chiefs as inducements to sell. After the revolutionary war, the immediate gain to be derived from land sales was of great importance to many Iroquois, who saw poverty descending upon them as the old way of life was fast disappearing.

But selling their land only made the Iroquois more dependent. As more and more non-Indians settled in the regions bordering on their territory and cleared the land for farming, the game animals moved farther away. Continued land sales thus made hunting more and more difficult for the Iroquois and led them to seek other sources of support. In the short run, all profited from the sale of land. In the long run, the Iroquois were selling their birthright and their independence, although they did not realize it at the time. Tiny reservations surrounded by a sea of non-Indians were all that was left of the once vast domain of the Six Nations Confederacy. With their land gone, their once awesome power was but a memory.

The division of the confederacy into Canadian (Grand River) and New York branches after the Revolution had weakened the old League. Its members were pushed apart by conflicting interests and by their respective relations with either United States or British officials. Factional disputes also arose on both sides of the border over League diplomacy and leadership issues. The League became unable to function as a unified whole.

By 1803, the Grand River Iroquois had transferred the council fire of the confederacy to the Onondaga village on their own reserve. The Iroquois on the American side still looked to Buffalo

Creek as their capital. The firekeeper there was an Onondaga named Uthawa, or Captain Cold. After Captain Cold's death in 1847, the council fire on the American side was moved back to the Onondaga reservation in central New York. The League became permanently divided, with a set of chiefs elected for each side of the border.

The political and military decline of the Iroquois Confederacy was accompanied by social decline on the reservations. In earlier times, the men had traveled widely to hunt, fight, and carry on diplomacy. Now the men had very little to do. Hunting was much restricted. The warriors could go to war only when and if they were needed as volunteers in the white man's army. Diplomacy was limited to a few leading men negotiating with representatives of the federal government or occasional embassies traveling to the United States capital. Only the women had a secure place in Iroquois society. They continued, as of old, to carry on with their traditional tasks as mothers, housekeepers, and farmers.

Longhouse of the Onondaga, keepers of the council fire, on the Six Nations Reserve. Living in both the United States and Canada, the Iroquois had two fires and two sets of chiefs.

The loss of morale and disintegrating conditions on the reservations resulted in idleness, chronic drunkenness, gossip, violent disputes, and family instability. The Iroquois had then reached the lowest point in their existence.

Certain non-Indians attempted to help the Iroquois make a transition to their new way of life on the reservation. The Philadelphia Quakers had been concerned about Indians for more than 100 years. In 1798, they directed their concern toward the Allegany Senecas living along the New York-Pennsylvania border. Rather than stressing their particular form of religion, the Quakers sent people to teach reading, writing, and arithmetic and the crafts and skills needed in a modern farming community. As the Quakers put it, they wanted to promote "the works of the handy workman." The Quakers also promoted their concept of morality and ideals of sobriety and a stable family life.

Cornplanter, the chief warrior of the Senecas, had for years been advocating that the Indians adopt the economic system of their non-Indian neighbors, including the idea of men working in agriculture. He therefore firmly supported the Quaker missionaries and their program.

Living in Cornplanter's village at the time was his half brother, the sachem chief Ganiodaiyo, or Handsome Lake. The chief was a well-known medicine man but was also a chronic and dissipated alcoholic. He took to his bed in

Captain Cold, Onondaga firekeeper at Buffalo Creek, the capital of the New York State Iroquois in the early 19th century.

May 1799, weakened in body and deathly ill from incessant drinking.

On the morning of June 15, as he was coming out of his cabin, he collapsed and was helped back to bed. The news spread fast that Handsome Lake was dying. As his relatives and friends

Handsome Lake preaching, holding a wampum belt. Jesse Cornplanter based this 1905 drawing on tradition and his observations at meetings of the Longhouse religion.

gathered by his bedside, he lay still, showing no signs of life. About half an hour later, the watchers noticed that he seemed to be breathing. Then they felt the beginning of a weak pulse. Finally, after two hours, he opened his eyes. To the wonder of all present, Handsome Lake began to relate a profound religious experience that he had just had.

He had seen a vision, he said. Three finely dressed messengers in ceremonial costume had come to him with a command from the Creator. They told him first that he was to choose his sister and her husband as his medicine persons. Then he was to attend the Strawberry Festival to be held the next day, when the people would give thanks for the ripening of this berry. There he was to preach the message of *Gaiwiio*, the Good Word. This message was to condemn whiskey, witchcraft, magic love potions of enticement that destroyed families, and the practice of abortion. Wrongdoers must confess and repent of their wickedness. Because Handsome Lake was still too weak to attend the ceremonial, Cornplanter preached his brother's message for him.

For the Iroquois, who placed much trust in dreams and visions, this message had a profound impact. It was the first of several visions that would come to Handsome Lake. It also led to the practice of a new religion by his people.

In the following months, Handsome Lake had other visions relating to moral and social reform. During these periods, he went into a trance and saw many wonders and gained much wisdom. He witnessed the punishment of the wicked in hell: Drunkards were drinking hot liquid metal; men who had beaten their wives were pounding on a burning female image; gamblers were playing with red-hot metal cards; witches were being dipped into a kettle whose contents boiled over; immoral individuals were suffering burning torments. He also traveled to the realm of the blessed, meeting the spirits of the good people he had known on earth, and learning in this happy land how families in his own village should live in peace. He was also instructed by the sacred messenger who accompanied him on his journey that Indians should continue to perform their traditional religious ceremonies, particularly the Mid-Winter Festival.

In yet another vision during a third trance period, Handsome Lake was told to have the Gaiwiio written down in a book to be preserved for all time. He was also instructed to carry the message to all the peoples of the Six Nations.

The grave of Handsome Lake on the Onondaga Reservation south of Syracuse, New York.

The Good Word began to bring reformation into the lives of the Senecas, particularly when Handsome Lake combined his religious teachings with an emphasis on loyal and affectionate family relations, abstinence from alcohol, and encouragement of men's participation in the agricultural economy. Handsome Lake's doctrine thus gave religious reinforcement to the social transformation that his brother Cornplanter and the Quakers were promoting.

The Gaiwiio as taught by Handsome Lake gradually spread to other reservations. During his lifetime it was known as the "New Religion," as distinct from the "Old Religion" of the Iroquois. Handsome Lake's teaching survives today, now known as the "Old Religion" or Longhouse religion. It is the faith of modern Iroquois traditionalists.

The Quakers were not the only Christian group working among the Iroquois in the 19th century. At Caugh-nawaga and St. Regis, the Catholics continued their missionary tradition. In addition to the Quakers, other Protestants with missionaries on Iroquois reservations included the Episcopalians, Baptists, Methodists, and the New York Missionary Society, an interdenominational Protestant group. The New York Missionary Society sent pastors and teachers to organize churches and schools on the Tuscarora Reservation in Niagara County and the Buffalo Creek Reservation. Like the Quakers, they

Visitors at the first council house on the Six Nation Reserve. Log cabin–type construction was typical of Iroquois houses and communal buildings in the 19th century.

stressed men's participation in agriculture and taught such domestic skills as sewing, spinning, and weaving.

The New York Missionary Society later merged with the United Foreign Missionary Society, a largely Presbyterian organization. This, in turn, still later merged with the Boston-based American Board of Commissioners for Foreign Missions, a Congregational church organization. The most noteworthy of the American Board missionaries was Asher Wright, preacher to the Senecas. He served faithfully for many years, not only as a religious teacher but also as a champion and protector of Indian rights. He also devised a writing system for the Seneca language using the English alphabet and edited a newspaper in the Seneca language.

Eleazar Williams, a Caughnawaga Indian who later lived at St. Regis, had settled among the Oneidas in 1816 and began preaching to them as an Episcopalian. He spoke fluent Oneida and was a spellbinding orator. In a short time, he converted most of the Oneidas to the Episcopalian faith. Hoping to establish an Iroquois empire in the west with himself as leader, Williams set forth a plan to sell all Oneida lands in New York and move to Wisconsin territory. Despite his persuasive powers, Williams's plan met with overwhelming opposition from the Oneidas. He was, however, backed by a few young Oneida warriors. With their support, he gained assistance from some members of Congress and the Ogden Land Company, which had the exclusive right in

Rev. Eleazar Williams, an outstanding Oneida orator, converted many to the Episcopalian faith. This is a copy of a painting by George Catlin.

New York State to buy Iroquois land. Their influence enabled Williams to purchase a large tract of land from the Menominee and Winnebago Indians in Wisconsin. In 1823, those Oneidas who supported the move left their New York land and, with Williams, began the emigration to their new reservation in the west, near Green Bay, Wisconsin.

Seneca children at a school in Ottawa County, Indian Territory (Oklahoma), 1887. The students attended the school from the first through the eighth grades.

From 1830 to 1846, the U.S. government had a policy of forcing all eastern Indians to move west of the Mississippi River in order to make their lands available for settlement by non-Indians. In 1831, as a result of this removal policy, the Iroquois of Ohio, mainly the Senecas and Cayugas, sold off their two reservations at Lewistown and Sandusky and moved southwest to Indian Territory (now the state of Oklahoma).

In 1838, the Ogden Land Company used fraud, bribery, alcohol, and forgery to negotiate the Treaty of Buffalo Creek. Despite revelations about the methods by which the treaty was negotiated, its terms were approved by Congress. It deprived the Senecas of all their remaining reservations and provided for removal of all New York Iroquois to Kansas. Both the Quakers and Asher Wright, the Senecas' missionary, publicized the fraud and fought for years to nullify the treaty. In 1842, the Allegany and Cattaraugus reservations were returned to the Senecas, but Buffalo Creek and Tonawanda remained lost. In 1857, after a long struggle, the Tonawanda Senecas were able to repurchase most of their reservation from the Ogden Land Company.

This would be the end of the assault on Iroquois lands until well into the next century. From the 1940's on, however, both New York State and the federal government would again begin confiscating large areas of the remaining reservations, this time for "public improvements": a dam, a reservoir, roads, and an enlarged waterway.

By the mid-19th century, the program of educating the Iroquois Indians in the ways of non-Indians was beginning to benefit them. Iroquois men were developing small but prosperous farms and were learning other practical skills such as carpentry. Children and even some adults were beginning to learn the basics of reading, writing, and arithmetic, making them more knowl-

edgeable in their business dealings with non-Indians. A few of the brightest Indian students were able to attend high-quality local private schools off the reservations. Some were even able to go to college.

One of the most remarkable of these young educated Indians was a Tonawanda Seneca named Ely S. Parker. Because of his education and his knowledge of English, the chiefs chose him as interpreter when they negotiated with New York State and U.S. officials. While browsing in an Albany bookstore on one of his diplomatic visits to the state capital, Parker met Lewis

The Seneca Indian School in Wyandotte, Oklahoma, 1902.

Lewis Henry Morgan published his first study of the Iroquois, written in collaboration with Ely Parker, in 1851.

Henry Morgan, a young lawyer from Aurora, New York. This chance meeting would grow into a lifelong friendship, changing the course of both men's lives.

Morgan had already been interested in the Iroquois and their customs and was therefore delighted to meet this 16-year-old Seneca. In future years, Parker served as Morgan's main informant, educating him on Iroquois customs and traditions. Parker also introduced Morgan to the elders and ritualists of the Senecas—people who were more knowledgeable than he about Iroquois customs. Morgan was the first to combine direct observation, in-depth interviewing, and the application of rigorous methods of scholarship to the study of another society's way of life. As a result of his study and research, Morgan wrote a number of articles and books on the Iroquois. Because of his great contribution, Morgan is often called "the father of American anthropology."

Ely Parker later studied law but was denied the right to practice because, as an Indian, he was not recognized as a United States citizen. Morgan then helped him to get a job with the builders of the Genesee Valley Canal, where he learned engineering. When the Civil War broke out, Parker enlisted in the Union army and rose to become a brigadier general. He served on General Ulysses S. Grant's staff and, because of his fine handwriting, became Grant's military secretary. It was Parker who wrote out the document of surrender that Confederate general Robert E. Lee signed at Appomattox Court House in 1865. After Grant was elected president, Parker became commissioner of Indian Affairs—the first Indian to serve in that post.

The Iroquois studies begun by Lewis Henry Morgan encouraged others to do research on these Indians. As a result, the Iroquois have become one of the most studied and written-about Indian tribal groups in the country. A number of Iroquois themselves have taken lifelong scholarly interest in their own culture and history. The best

Ely Parker (seated, far right) was military secretary to General Ulysses S. Grant (standing, center) during the Civil War. Parker's friend John Rawlins (seated, far left) was Grant's chief of staff.

known of these are Arthur C. Parker, Ely S. Parker's grandnephew, and John N. B. Hewitt, a Tuscarora. Arthur Parker had a long and distinguished career first as an archaeologist with the New York State Museum in Albany and then as director of the Rochester Museum. Hewitt's career was equally distinguished. He was for many years an ethnologist at the Smithsonian Institution in Washington, D.C., and published an enormous amount of scholarly material on the Iroquois.

The Longhouse traditionalists still living on today's reservations and the Iroquois scholars of past years have done much to keep alive knowledge of the language, history, and customs of the People of the Extended Lodge. The traditionalists and scholars both have preserved a precious heritage for the generations who will follow them. ▲

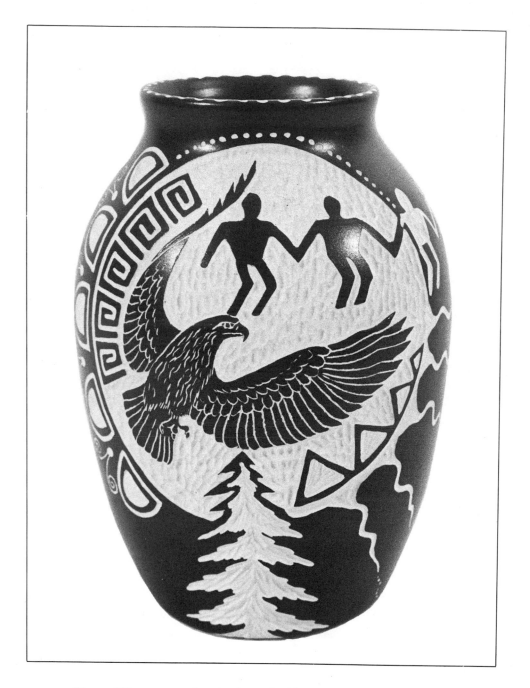

Tree of Peace *pot, clay, by Steve Smith, Mohawk, Six Nations Reserve, 1982. The artist shows the most important symbols of the League of the Iroquois: the pine tree of peace and the eagle flying above it. The figures holding hands represent the Six Nations of the League.*

THE
MODERN
IROQUOIS

As the 19th century progressed, the Iroquois made a successful transition from female-practiced to male-practiced agriculture. Other customs began to change as well. In the old days, the Iroquois had lived in bark longhouses, each of which contained an expanded or extended family. That usually meant an older married woman with her married daughters, their husbands, and their children. Iroquois women, as the farmers, had always played a key role in the traditional community economy. The land belonged to them. With the growing predominance of male-practiced agriculture, it became the tendency to move into separate family houses built in non-Indian style. The smaller, male-dominated family (father, mother, and children) now became the normal Iroquois pattern, the same as it was among rural non-Indians.

Land, once the possession of the women, now became the possession of men as it was bought and sold by male farmers. Although all reservation land belonged to the nation inhabiting that reservation and could not legally be sold to non-Indians, the Iroquois began to accept the right of private ownership of the soil by individuals or families and the right of inheritance of land. Individual Iroquois who owned land they did not or could not farm sometimes rented it out to other Indians or even to non-Indian farmers. In many ways, the Iroquois in the 19th century were approaching the patriarchal (male-dominated) pattern of their non-Indian neighbors.

In 1848, the Senecas of the Cattaraugus and Allegany reservations had a quiet revolution. These Senecas had become very dissatisfied over the way the chiefs dispensed the annuity payments that came to them from the federal government as a result of the 1794 Treaty of Canandaigua between the United States and the Six Nations on the U.S. side of the border. These annuities consisted of a yearly payment of $4,500, largely in trade goods. The payments

Seneca women's nomination wampum belt. The six linked figures represent the Six Nations, and the rectangle symbolizes Onondaga, the capital of the confederacy. In 1898 the council of the Onondaga Nation voted to give the University of the State of New York "full power to get possession and safely keep forever all wampums" of the League. But some Iroquois today believe that the wampum should be returned to them.

were to be apportioned among those tribal groups living in New York State that had signed the treaty.

Most of these New York Senecas wanted the payments made directly to the heads of families, rather than having the chiefs take a portion out first for general governmental expenses on these reservations. Also, the people still harbored grievances against the chiefs for signing the Treaty of Buffalo Creek in 1838, which had deprived them of a tremendous amount of land. As a result, they overthrew the hereditary chiefs and set up an elective councillor system under a written constitution. Henceforth, these two reservations would be known as the Seneca Nation. In imitation of the governing system of their non-Indian neighbors, the Seneca Nation deprived its women of the right to vote. It was not until 1964 that the women of the Seneca Nation secured the right to vote in tribal elections.

The Tonawanda Senecas, who had never recognized the Treaty of Buffalo Creek, retained their original form of government, with hereditary chiefs chosen by the senior women of each clan. These two divisions in government exist to this day between the Seneca Nation (Allegany and Cattaraugus) and the more traditionalist Tonawanda Band of Senecas.

The St. Regis Mohawk Reservation was located both south and north of the St. Lawrence River, in New York State and in the provinces of Quebec and Ontario in Canada. The Mohawks on the United States side had adopted an elective system of government in 1802. Originally there were three elected "trustees." Later this number was expanded to 12, and the elected officials were called chiefs.

In the 20th century, the Longhouse religion of Handsome Lake was established on the Caughnawaga Reservation in the 1920s and on the St. Regis Reservation in the 1930s. This religious group has revived the old hereditary chief system and on both reservations these chiefs now exist in opposition to the elective chiefs who govern the reserves.

The Six Nations Reserve in Canada had maintained a hereditary chief system throughout the 19th century. The Canadian government, however, imposed a patrilineal form of descent (according to the father's family line) on all Indian groups in Canada. To the matrilineal Iroquois (descending according to the mother's family line), this has caused no end of confusion, for it affects tribal membership and even throws clan membership into doubt.

In 1924, as a result of a political upheaval on the Six Nations Reserve, an elective council was established. It is

Chiefs at Six Nations Reserve with wampum belts, 1871. From left: Joseph Snow, Onondaga; George Johnson, Mohawk, interpreter; John Buck, Onondaga, wampum keeper; John Smoke Johnson, Mohawk, council speaker; Isaac Hill, Onondaga, firekeeper; Seneca Johnson, Seneca.

currently the recognized form of government. The hereditary chiefs appointed by clan mothers continue to function, largely in a ritual capacity connected with the various longhouses of the Handsome Lake religion on the reserve. In 1959 and again in 1970, the hereditary chiefs' faction and their followers attempted to seize control of the reservation government, but failed.

Today only three reservations—Onondaga, Tonawanda, and Tuscarora—all in New York, are governed by the old traditional system of hereditary chiefs. The clan mothers of the respec-

tive tribal clans still nominate the chiefs for their clan, and these men are then raised to office by means of the ancient Condolence Council.

The Oneidas of Wisconsin lost a tremendous amount of land as a result of the General Allotment Act of 1887. This legislation was an attempt by the United States government to destroy the tribal form of society in the West, by breaking up the reservations into small parcels of land that were then given, or allotted, to individual Indians. The Indians were to become farmers and citizens and thus more readily as-

Lacrosse team at Onondaga, 1902. In lacrosse, a game of American Indian origin, a hard rubber ball is caught, carried, and passed in the basketlike head of a stick called a crosse.

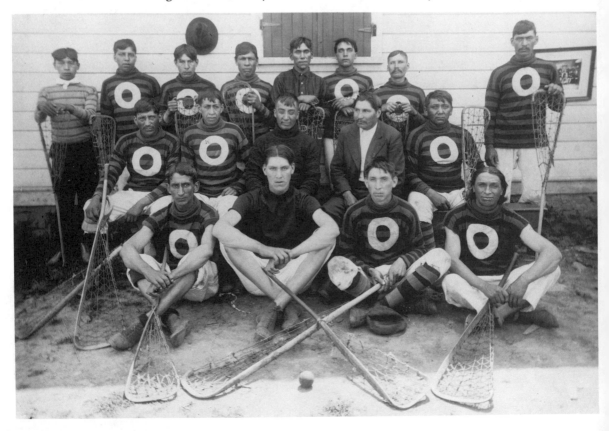

Oneida farm boy, Wisconsin, 1901. The Oneidas in Wisconsin lost a great deal of their land when they were unable to raise the cash needed to pay local taxes.

similate into the general population. Once their land had been taken out of federal protective status and given to them for private ownership, however, the Oneidas were unable to pay the local and county taxes that were levied on these allotments. As a result, they saw almost all of their reservation land taken away from them. Their tribal government also fell apart.

Indians continued to lose their land as a result of the General Allotment Act until there was a change in government policy in the late 1920s and 1930s. The Indian Reorganization Act of 1934 was of particular importance in beginning to solve the Wisconsin Oneidas' problems. They took advantage of the provisions of this law to form a new government, write a constitution, and incorporate the tribe. Under their new government, Oneida men and women both could vote and hold office. The federal government also repurchased some additional land for the tribe.

The Indian Reorganization Act was a new beginning for the Oneidas. They established a number of business enterprises on the Wisconsin reservation and have also built a home for their senior citizens and the Oneida Museum to preserve their heritage. Today, their leaders are well educated and capable, and after many years of struggle the community has begun to prosper.

Whether in Wisconsin, Oklahoma, New York, Quebec, or Ontario, most reservation Iroquois today live in much the same way as neighboring rural non-Indians. Although many still maintain vegetable gardens for their own use, most Iroquois are no longer farmers. The small amount of land they possess and the large financial outlay needed for modern farm machinery put full-time farming beyond the means of most Iroquois. The men today prefer construction work and factory employment and usually commute daily from their reservations to work. They are particularly noted as ironworkers, traveling throughout the United States to construct skyscrapers and bridges. Women

IROQUOIS LOCATIONS TODAY

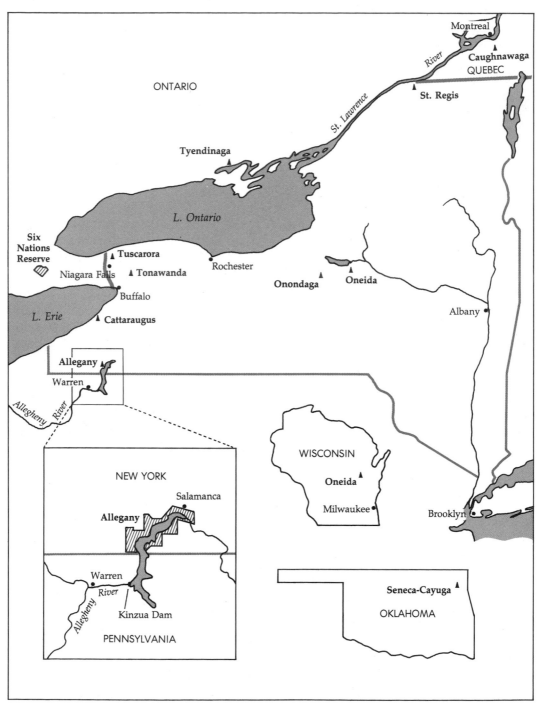

also often work off the reservation in a variety of occupations.

Many Iroquois have moved more or less permanently to the cities where employment is available. The largest nonreservation Iroquois populations in New York State cities are in Buffalo, Niagara Falls, Rochester, and the borough of Brooklyn in New York City, where many St. Regis and Caughnawaga people have moved. Many Oneidas live in Milwaukee, Wisconsin.

An increasing number of young Iroquois men and women complete high school and go on to colleges and universities, where they often study such professions as teaching, social work, law, and medicine. A few Iroquois have also gone into state and federal government service, some reaching high-level posts. In 1966, Robert L. Bennett, an Oneida from Wisconsin, was appointed commissioner of Indian Affairs. He was followed in that post from 1969 to 1972 by Louis R. Bruce, Jr., of St. Regis Mohawk and Oglala Sioux ancestry.

During much of the 20th century, the Iroquois have suffered continual attacks on their rights, their independence, and their land base. One such denial of their rights followed passage of the Immigration Act of 1924. One section of this act said: "No alien ineligible to citizenship shall be admitted to the United States." Because of American prejudices in the period, this provision was specifically intended to keep Asians out of the country. Immigration officials also applied the ban to Indians attempting to cross the border from Canada. Because so many Indians had been accustomed to crossing the border freely to visit friends and family and to work, this policy was a serious blow. Concerned Iroquois fought this interpretation of the act on both moral and legal grounds.

The Jay Treaty of 1794 between the United States and Great Britain had specifically permitted "the Indians dwelling on either side of said boundary line, freely to pass and repass" into each country. Paul K. Diabo, a Caughnawaga Mohawk who was now prevented from coming into the United States to work at his usual job, hired a Philadelphia law firm to fight his case for him. Clinton Rickard, a Tuscarora living on the Tuscarora Reservation near Niagara Falls, fought the Immigration Act by informing sympathetic non-Indians about the effects of the act, forming the Indian Defense League of America with other concerned Indians in 1927, and lobbying Congress. Diabo's and Rickard's efforts eventually succeeded. The courts recognized the supremacy of the Jay Treaty, and Congress in 1928 specifically provided for uninterrupted Indian passage over the border.

The Indian Defense League of America is the oldest ongoing Indian rights group in the United States and continues to fight injustice against Indians. It also preserves a special celebration held every year on the third Saturday in July. The Border Crossing Celebration commemorates the victory gained in 1928. "Border Crossing" has become a general Indian Day in the Niagara Falls area, where Indians from the cities and reservations gather in colorful costumes for a parade across the border and a picnic at a nearby park, with sports, speeches by dignitaries, displays of Indian dancing, the sale of Indian crafts, and general assertions of pride in being Indian.

Shortly after World War II, in the late 1940s and 1950s, the U.S. government decided to end its involvement in Indian affairs. This meant the end of federal responsibility for Indians, removal of Indian lands from federal trust status, and nullification, or "termination," of the many treaties with the various Indian tribes. The plan included a "relocation" program by which the Bureau of Indian Affairs (BIA) urged Indians throughout the country to leave the reservations and move to cities. BIA officials offered every Indian a one-way ticket to a city where the BIA had an office that could help the newcomer find housing and work. The object was to move as many Indians as possible off the reservations and eventually to close down the bureau itself. The government called this policy "freeing the Indians." Under this program, the government terminated federally recognized status for 109 Indian groups. The termination program succeeded primarily in "freeing" the Indians from their land and plunging them into deeper poverty.

The New York Iroquois united in a vigorous struggle to fight termination. They partially succeeded. The federal treaties with the Iroquois still stand, but civil and criminal legal jurisdiction over the Iroquois have been turned over to New York State. The Oneidas of Wisconsin and the Seneca-Cayugas of Oklahoma also fought doggedly against the termination of their status and were eventually successful.

The next attacks were against Iroquois land, and the Indians consistently lost.

In the 1950s the Army Corps of Engineers, over the strong objection of the Senecas, proposed to build a dam near Warren, Pennsylvania, for flood-control purposes. When completed, the Kinzua Dam would flood the entire Cornplanter Reservation in Pennsylvania and large sections of the Allegany Reservation in New York. The building of this dam would thus have been in violation of the Treaty of Canandaigua of 1794 in which the United States guaranteed the Iroquois safe possession of their land.

The Senecas conducted a major campaign against the dam through the newspapers and television, in the courts, and by lobbying Congress and Pennsylvania and New York State officials. They gained the support of many non-Indian religious and civil liberties organizations as well as that of other Indian nations across the country. Cornelius Seneca, George Heron, and Basil Williams, each of whom served as president of the Seneca Nation at various times during these years of struggle, led their people in a determined battle to preserve their land.

Seneca Indian leaders George D. Heron (left) and Sidney Carney in 1964 look out at land on the Cornplanter Reservation that would be flooded by construction of the Kinzua Dam.

The Seneca Nation hired Dr. Arthur E. Morgan as consulting engineer. Morgan, who had formerly headed the Tennessee Valley Authority, worked with Barton M. Jones, who had been the chief designing engineer of that vast flood control project. They drew up an alternate plan that would be more effective for flood control and would preserve Indian lands. The Army Corps of Engineers was uninterested in Morgan's plan and the government went ahead with the construction of the Kinzua Dam.

The completed dam resulted in the flooding of more than 9,000 acres of Seneca land, necessitating the removal of 130 Seneca families and the relocation of Seneca graves to a safe location. This disruption of their lives caused profound shock to the Senecas. Even today, those who went through this shattering experience cannot speak of it without deep emotion and overwhelming grief.

The government compensated the Seneca Nation financially for the loss of their land. The Senecas put the money to good use by building two community centers—one on each reserve—and setting up a scholarship fund. But to the Senecas, their land was far more important. Land is forever, but money is soon gone.

A four-year-old Tuscarora took a turn on the picket line protesting the seizure of reservation land for a reservoir in 1958.

Between 1958 and 1960, the Tuscaroras fought an attempt by the New York State Power Authority to confiscate a large portion of their reservation near Niagara Falls for a reservoir. Considering their land more valuable than money, the chiefs' council, under Chief Elton Greene, turned down a large monetary offer and instead took the case through the courts all the way to the United States Supreme Court. While the case was still pending in the courts, the State Power Authority sent personnel onto the reservation to begin work. The men and women of the tribe united in a militant mass obstruction of this invasion, standing in front of surveyors' stakes, lying down in front of trucks, carrying protest signs, and engaging in heated arguments with the workers. One 14-year-old boy took his rifle and shot a stake out of a surveyor's hand, demonstrating the skill that Indian men and boys continue to develop as hunters. The State Power Authority then called in well-armed police to protect them as they dug up the reservation.

On March 7, 1960, the Supreme Court rendered a split decision of four to three against the Tuscaroras. The Indians had lost, but both they and their cause had received wide publicity throughout the country. The militant demonstrations they had carried on for months while their case was in the courts were the beginning of a new tactic in Indian protest movements. This tactic would be relied on by other Indians across the country in future years.

The Caughnawaga and St. Regis reservations also suffered significant land losses when the St. Lawrence Seaway was enlarged in the late 1950s. Both Canada and the United States ignored treaties and Indian land rights in the interest of industrial development. These governments' idea of progress had little room for Indians.

It is often difficult for non-Indians to understand the deep attachment that Indians feel for their land. For the Iroquois, their reservations are the only lands they have retained as their own after years of pressure to separate them from the millions of acres that were once theirs. Preservation of their current landholdings, the relatively few acres left, means the preservation of their communities, their heritage, and their identity. The reservations are home, the place where Indians can be themselves, practice their customs, their religion, their way of life. Upon their own land, among their own people, the Iroquois Indians are most truly themselves. Even those who live in the cities return frequently to the reservation to see relatives and friends and be spiritually refreshed.

In their own communities, the Iroquois retain their sovereignty and their independence. They can govern themselves and preserve their own sense of worth. Even though they have lived for nearly 200 years in close proximity to non-Indians, they have preserved their attachment to Indian values. They take from outsiders what is of benefit to them, what will make their lives better;

Clinton Rickard formed the Indian Defense League of America in 1927, when he led the struggle against unjust provisions of the 1924 Immigration Act.

but most Iroquois have no wish to assimilate and thus lose their own unique identity. They are proud of their Indianness and proud of being contemporary representatives of the Kanonghsionni, the Extended Lodge of the Iroquois Founding Fathers. ▲

BIBLIOGRAPHY

Armstrong, William H. *Warrior in Two Camps: Ely S. Parker, Union General and Seneca Chief.* Syracuse, NY: Syracuse University Press, 1978.

Cornplanter, Jesse J. *Legends of the Longhouse.* Port Washington, NY: Ira J. Friedman, 1963.

Hale, Horatio, ed. *The Iroquois Book of Rites.* Introduction by William N. Fenton. Toronto: University of Toronto Press, 1963.

Hauptman, Laurence M. *The Iroquois Struggle for Survival: World War II to Red Power.* Syracuse, NY: Syracuse University Press, 1986.

Henry, Thomas R. *Wilderness Messiah: The Story of Hiawatha and the Iroquois.* New York: William Sloane Associates, 1955.

Hertzberg, Hazel W. *The Great Tree and the Longhouse: The Culture of the Iroquois.* New York: Macmillan, 1966.

Kelsay, Isabel Thompson. *Joseph Brant, 1743–1807: Man of Two Worlds.* Syracuse, NY: Syracuse University Press, 1984.

Lenski, Lois. *Indian Captive: The Story of Mary Jemison.* Philadelphia: Lippincott, 1941.

Lyford, Carrie A. *Iroquois Crafts.* Washington, D.C.: U.S. Department of the Interior–Bureau of Indian Affairs, n.d.

Morgan, Lewis Henry. *League of the Ho-De-No Sau-Nee or Iroquois.* 2 vols. New Haven, CT: Human Relations Area Files, 1954.

Parker, Arthur C. *Parker on the Iroquois.* Edited by William N. Fenton. Syracuse, NY: Syracuse University Press, 1968.

Rickard, Clinton. *Fighting Tuscarora: The Autobiography of Chief Clinton Rickard.* Edited by Barbara Graymont. Syracuse, NY: Syracuse University Press, 1973.

Wallace, Anthony F. C. *The Death and Rebirth of the Seneca.* New York: Knopf, 1970.

———. "Dreams and Wishes of the Soul; A Type of Psychoanalytic Theory Among the Seventeenth Century Iroquois." *American Anthropologist* 60 (March 1958): 234-248.

Wallace, Paul A. W. *The White Roots of Peace*. Port Washington, NY: Ira J. Friedman, 1968.

THE IROQUOIS AT A GLANCE

TRIBES *Mohawk, Oneida, Onondaga, Cayuga, Seneca, Tuscarora*

CULTURE AREA *Northeast*

ORIGINAL GEOGRAPHY *Upstate New York, south of Lake Ontario*

PRESENT RESERVATIONS *New York State, Quebec, Ontario, Wisconsin, Oklahoma*

LINGUISTIC FAMILY *Iroquoian*

CURRENT POPULATION *About 55,000*

FIRST CONTACT *Jacques Cartier, French, 1534, St. Lawrence Iroquois groups; Samuel de Champlain, French, 1609, New York Iroquois*

FEDERAL STATUS *Recognized*

GLOSSARY

Algonkian The Indian people living in the northeastern United States and east-central Canada whose languages are related and who share numerous cultural characteristics.

Algonquian The languages spoken by most Indian peoples in northeastern North America, including those who geographically surrounded the Iroquois.

Algonquins A tribal group living in the Ottawa River valley region of Canada. In colonial times, they were an important ally of France.

anthropology The study of the physical, social, and cultural characteristics of human beings.

blood feud Violent acts of retaliation between individuals and families resulting in ongoing revenge.

clan A group in American Indian society that traces its descent, either actually or theoretically, from a common ancestor. Membership in a clan establishes membership in a tribe. Among the Iroquois, descent and consequently clan membership are traced through the mother's line only.

culture The total learned behavior and ways of thinking of human beings; the socially transmitted, nonbiological activities that constitute the way of life of a given group of people.

culture area A geographical region in which the cultures of a number of tribes or other groups share numerous traits or elements.

exorcism The process of driving out or expelling an evil spirit from an afflicted individual.

Iroquoian A large group of separate tribal peoples in the Northeast and Carolina regions speaking related languages and having similar cultures. Most were eventually conquered or incorporated by the Six Nations. Also, the languages spoken by these tribal groups.

Iroquois The Iroquoian people; specifically, the Six Nations: Mohawk, Oneida, Onondaga, Cayuga, Seneca, Tuscarora.

Jesuit A member of the Society of Jesus, a Roman Catholic religious order founded by Ignatius Loyola in 1534. The Jesuits were highly learned and active in spreading the faith.

lineage A group of individuals related through descent from a common ancestor; a descent group whose members recognize as relatives people on the mother's side only or the father's side only.

matchlock An old form of portable firearm having a burning wick (match) for firing the priming powder.

matrilineal descent Relationship traced through the mother's line.

nation A term used generally by the early Europeans in North America to describe the Indian tribal societies they encountered. Broadly, any large group of people having similar institutions, language, customs, and political and social ties.

ohwachira A basic political and social unit in the Iroquois clan comprising all the male and female children of a leading woman and all the descendants of her female children. One or more *ohwachiras* constituted a clan. Certain *ohwachiras* within a clan held the right to chiefship titles.

patrilineal descent Relationship traced through the father's line.

Quakers The familiar name for members of the Religous Society of Friends, a mystical and pacifist group founded in England by George Fox in the 17th century. Quakers were active in efforts to help Indians during the 19th century.

relocation The attempt on the part of the federal government to encourage Indians to leave the tribal environment of the reservation and migrate to the cities in order to enter mainstream society.

reservation Indian homelands either set aside by the United States or Canadian governments or retained by Indians as a result of past treaty negotiations; land designated for occupation by and the use of Indians. In Canada they are usually called reserves.

sachem A tribal ruler or chief. The word comes from the Narragansett dialect of New England and was applied by Europeans to chiefs of non-Iroquois tribes in the Northeast. When applied to the Iroquois, it refers to the hereditary civil or peace chiefs, the "lords" of the Confederacy.

shaman A person who has special powers to call on spirit beings and mediate between the supernatural world and the world of ordinary people. The word comes from the Tungus language of Siberia.

squatters Persons who occupy and live on a plot of land without having legal title to it.

state A form of social and politcal organization embracing a territory and having laws supported by force and sanctions. People in a state society are divided into social and economic classes, privileged and subordinate groups.

termination The removal of Indian tribes from federal government supervision and Indian lands from federal trust status. The policy was initiated by Congress during the presidencies of Harry S. Truman and Dwight D. Eisenhower.

tribe A type of society consisting of several or many separate communities bound together by common language, territory, and culture. A tribe's communities are united by kinship and such social units as clans, religious organizations, and economic and political institutions. They generally lack a centralized government that can enforce political decisions.

wampum Shell beads used by the Iroquois in strings or "belts" as a pledge of the truth of their words, symbols of high office, records of diplomatic negotiations and treaties, and records of other important events. From the Algonquian word *wampumpeag*, meaning white (bead) strings.

witchcraft The practice of doing harm to others by use of black, or evil, magic.

INDEX

PICTURE CREDITS

American Museum of Natural History, page 83 *right*; American Numismatic Society, page 89; AP/Wide World Photos, pages 81, 117, 118; Art Resource, page 47; The Bettmann Archive, pages 27, 46, 84; Bibliothèque National/Giraudon/Art Resource, page 48; Cranbrook Institute of Science, pages 15, 37, 40, 41, 50, 51 *inset*, 53 *left inset*, 56; Culver Pictures, page 107; Giraudon/Art Resource, pages 76, 77; Barbara Graymont, page 86; Carmelo Guadagno/Museum of the American Indian, Heye Foundation, pages 14, 25; Metropolitan Toronto Library Board, page 90; Museum of the American Indian, Heye Foundation, pages 49, 50 *inset*, 54, 55, 62, 68; National Archives of Canada, pages 66, 83 *left*; The New-York Historical Society, pages 64, 87, 88, 92; New York State Historical Association, pages 74, 93; New York State Library, pages 39, 56 *inset*, 100; New York State Museum, cover, pages 29, 43, 61, 72, 110; Onondaga County Department of Parks and Recreation, pages 101, 112; private collection, pages 52, 53; courtesy of Clinton Rickard Family, page 119; Rochester Museum and Science Center (height 50.8 cm, width 38.1 cm), page 22; Schoharie Museum of the Iroquois Indian, pages 12, 16, 18, 20, 28, 34, 36, 44, 52 *inset*, 69, 108; Smithsonian Institution, pages 21, 31, 32, 53 *right inset*, 96, 111; Smithsonian Institution National Anthropological Archives, pages 98, 102, 113; Snark International/Art Resource, page 59; State Historical Society of Wisconsin, page 103; University of Oklahoma Library, Western History Collections, pages 104, 105; University of Rochester Library, page 106; Yale University, page 99.

Maps (pages 2, 60, 70, 79, 95, 114) by Gary Tong.

BARBARA GRAYMONT, a historian and leading authority on the Iroquois Indians, received a Ph.D. in history from Columbia University. She is professor of history at Nyack College, Nyack, New York, and previously taught at Bates College, Lewiston, Maine. Dr. Graymont is the author of numerous books and articles, including several volumes in the series *Early American Indian Documents.* Her book *The Iroquois in the American Revolution* was cited as a source in a 1985 Supreme Court decision that upheld a land claim of the Oneida Indian Nation. For many years she has spent summers living and working among the Tuscarora Indians of upstate New York, researching and writing about their history and culture. She has been involved in Indian rights movements and is an honorary member of the Indian Defense League of America.

FRANK W. PORTER III, General Editor of INDIANS OF NORTH AMERICA, is Director of the Chelsea House Foundation for American Indian Studies. He holds a B.A., M.A., and Ph.D. from the University of Maryland. He has done extensive research concerning the Indians of Maryland and Delaware and is the author of numerous articles on their history, archaeology, geography, and ethnography. He was formerly Director of the Maryland Commission on Indian Affairs and American Indian Research and Resource Institute, Gettysburg, Pennsylvania, and he has received grants from the Delaware Humanities Forum, the Maryland Committee for the Humanities, the Ford Foundation, and the National Endowment for the Humanities, among others. Dr. Porter is the author of *The Bureau of Indian Affairs* in the Chelsea House KNOW YOUR GOVERNMENT series.